SOFT SOULS LIVING
IN A HARSH WORLD

TIM URSINY, PHD,
AND JAMIE URSINY, MIT

SoftSouls.com

Published by Advantage Coaching & Training, Inc.
480 E. Roosevelt Road, West Chicago, Illinois 60185
(630) 293-0210
www.advantagecoaching.com

Printed and bound in the United States of America.
POD

To KP-Ski, Toad, Jamie Wee-Wee, and Ferkle. In our hearts,
you will always be innocent and have a joy for life.

To Frances Knight, who, despite a harsh world, always believed in and loved her children.
She gave her children the gift of loving souls and the faith to live in a world that is not
always so kind.

To Andrew Knight, for his kindness, patience, and support over the years.

To Kenneth Richard Ursiny, who will always be loved as a father.

CONTENTS

ACKNOWLEDGMENTS

WE WOULD LIKE TO DEDICATE THIS BOOK TO ALL OF THE SOFT SOULS OUT there. Our hearts go out to your hearts, and we hope this book speaks to the depths of your souls.

We would like to thank Marla Ursiny, Carole Smith, Susan Gage, Carole Cowperthwaite-O'Hagan, Steve Johnson, Lisa Kueng, Beth Fawcett, Carlos and Linda Vergara, Tony DiLeonardi, David Goetz, Peter Lynch, David Bell, Julie Bosher Chavez, Justin Johanson, Alissa Ursiny, and Kelly Brady for their input, proofreading, and support for our mission.

Our deepest appreciation to Carolyn Hewett, who goes above and beyond as a therapist, a friend, and an amazing prayer partner. Most of all, we would like to thank Jacki Jochum, Samantha Jochum, Kyle Ursiny, Hunter Nicole Wilson, Zach Ursiny, Colton Ursiny, and Vance Ursiny for giving this book meaning. May your soft souls always be a blessing to those around you.

PART ONE

UNDERSTANDING THE SOFT SOUL

HOW TO NAVIGATE THIS BOOK

W E WILL BE TAKING AN UNUSUAL JOURNEY IN THE WRITING STYLE OF THIS book in order to create a deep emotional understanding of the soft soul—part memoir, part self-help. This is an unusual combination, and at times, it may feel like you are reading two different books. However, we did this purposely, because we feel that the combination of these is critical to fully understand the blessings, dilemmas, and solutions that come with being a soft soul. The first section of this book will set up the premise of the soft soul and explore what makes someone a soft soul. The second part is focused on how soft souls cope with the harshness of the world differently. In our third section, we will concentrate on ways to heal, protect, and recharge your soft soul, and then in the final section, we will bring closure to the stories presented earlier.

The chapters in the second section will alternate between true interconnected stories of six soft souls journeying through this harsh world and brief chapters that describe the specific coping styles shown in these stories. These coping styles represent universal ways that human beings try to adapt to the challenges of the world. While there are additional ways that soft souls cope with the world, we believe that many of you will identify with the Idealist, the Charmer, the Fighter, the Pleaser, the Invisible One, or the Addicted One. We know these six soft souls and their coping styles very well, because they are our family members, and this is our story. And while these individuals do not represent all of the ways soft souls cope with this tough world, they do represent six distinct ways of trying to successfully and unsuccessfully protect ourselves from the challenges of the world. We wanted to share our story, because one of the most powerful gifts that someone can give us is to help us understand that we are not alone. We find that out best by sharing life experiences. By relating to others who have suffered similar things and have overcome them, we can often find understanding and hope. Since these stories are true, a few names have been changed and information omitted that may hurt other people.

As mentioned, between the story chapters, we will share general characteristics of each type of protective or coping style to help you identify your own style, and then we will give some brief suggestions for that particular style of protection. We will be focusing these chapters mostly on the *ways of adapting* to the harsh world rather than the *type of soft soul*, because we can influence the ways that we adapt. We can't fully control the pains we experience in the world or our natural predispositions, but we *can* control the choices we make as we navigate our experiences. Basically, our genetic makeup plus our life experiences plus our choices determine who we become later in life. However, you cannot control your genetic makeup, and you cannot control your past life experiences, but you can control your choices. So that is where we will focus in our self-help chapters.

We know that many of you will see your own lives and experiences in these stories, and the second section may, at times, be painful for some of you to read. *Do not* stop after the stories! The third section of the book will bring hope out of the pain and guidance for navigating this tough world. Through our experiences as a psychologist and a teacher, we will discuss various successful strategies for integrating your soft soul together with ways to protect yourself so that no part of who you are needs to be sacrificed or damaged. This section is about healing and protecting your soft soul and is loaded with practical tactics that you can implement immediately to aid you on your journey.

Then, in our final chapter, you will catch up with the family of soft souls and discover how they survived the challenges. However, if you are in a very difficult place in life and the stories are too painful, feel free to simply jump to the conceptual chapters and/or to the third section of the book and discover ways to work through your own journey.

We pray that this book caresses your spirit and helps you truly honor your soft soul. We also hope it gives ideas for finding your inner strength while staying true to the beautiful, loving, tender person you were meant to be. We hope that your soft soul finds encouragement in the stories of people just like you who have fought to survive and thrive in a hard, harsh world.

CHAPTER 1

....

BORN SOFT

WE ARE ALL BORN PHYSICALLY SOFT, WITH ALL THOSE VELVETY LITTLE DIMPLES that no one can resist stroking and caressing while cooing and making funny faces. Everyone adores our physical softness, even envies it. Parents spend hours trying to preserve that baby smoothness; they wash, dry, and lotion, wash, dry, and lotion, almost to obsession. However, there is a different kind of softness that we are born with that has nothing to do with our exteriors but rather with a softness and purity of spirit. This internal softness shows up in our laughter, our smiles, and our desire to be held and nurtured. Later in life, it is still evident in many of us, showing up as gentleness, kindness, deep passion, and a longing for peace and fairness. It is sensitivity to our feelings and to the feelings of others, a compassion for humanity, and a desire for harmony. Softness within the spirit is the natural ability to trust, the willingness to love unselfishly, and the deepest desire to be loved and accepted. Who could complain about those?

So why is it that we do not all celebrate our soft natures, our compassion, our desire to do right even when wronged? It is partly because, at least in the Western world, we live in a society where softness can be considered not just a weakness but a serious defect of character. Think of all the negative terms a person can call you. Many people consider "weak" or "soft" to be among the worst. In the world's thinking, a strong person is a person who never allows anyone to take advantage of them, hurt them, or give them less than they deserve. A strong person is a person whose soul cannot be penetrated.

We believe that many (and perhaps even all) of us are born soft on the outside *and* on the inside. Our spirits come into this world soft, but do not mistake softness for weakness. They are not the same. Those who have seen a three-pound premature baby fighting for his or her life know the human spirit does not come into this world weak. Anyone who has seen a kind person forgive someone for deeply hurting him or her knows the incredible strength of the soft soul. Anyone who has seen loving people risk their lives to bring food and supplies after a natural disaster knows the phenomenal impact that soft souls can have on others and the world.

So where does this misconception begin? It is a lesson we typically learn from those who love us most—the good, caring people who only have our best interests at heart. Go to any playground, and you will eventually hear a well-meaning parent say to a child who has fallen down or been shunned by friends, "Come on. You're tough. Don't cry. You can take it. Be a grown-up girl. Be a big boy!" Our children go to schools every day where they are teased and subjected to daily abuse, and wonderful, loving parents or teachers say, "You have to stop being so sensitive." The message: "Stop being a soft soul."

On the other hand, other parents may try to control their child's exposure to any self-esteem challenges from others by controlling their environments. Rather than teaching their child how to be who they are and maintain their self-worth despite others' opinions, they demand that their child never be exposed to disapproval. Examples of this are seen at ball games where parents are not allowed to cheer for their child's team for fear it may upset the children on the losing team or in contests where everyone gets a medal so no one feels left out. Sadly, both hardness and overprotection are false solutions. Hardness is a manufactured force field that *may* keep away the hurt, but it can also keep out the love, joy, and passion. The "no one loses" approach does not prepare us for a world that is often competitive and tough. One approach simply hides us from the pain, leaving us removed from the human race (and sometimes even from ourselves); the other only protects us on a very short-term basis. The long-term impact for both is that, in our quiet and most alone moments, soft souls still feel the hurt and the pain, and they feel they must suffer alone.

Another reason we do not tend to celebrate our soft natures is due to our overall experiences with the world. When our softness is greeted by a safe and functional environment, we can grow up expressing these deep feelings and developing strong and compassionate personalities; when we experience a harsh and dysfunctional environment, we have to develop ways to protect ourselves from the pain of the world. The degrees of challenge we experience in life can vary greatly, and the greater the pain, the more likely our protective strategies become overused. For some, those strategies that protected them well in childhood are still being used later in life in situations that don't require them, and those strategies can now cause dysfunction and pain. Protection that helps us at one stage or in one part of our lives can hurt us at another. For example, police officers are taught that, when responding to a domestic violence situation, they should be suspicious and mistrusting of everyone. This "paranoia" saves their lives, because often, they are lied to and would be incredibly vulnerable to harm if they were too trusting. That protective device is appropriate for that situation. However, if they bring that same protective style to their personal lives with their families, that same "paranoia" can be incredibly harmful to relationships. What protects them in one situation can hurt them in another. In their personal lives, it would be helpful to adapt that protective style and merge it with their soft, loving, and trusting souls.

Without a safe environment and proper guidance, soft souls may seek out unhealthy ways to hide from life's pain. Many ease their internal suffering by constantly seeking the love and approval of others. They often tolerate unspeakable situations and accept multiple abuses to gain love and achieve peace at any cost. Others simply hide from the world and refuse to face reality. They live life through rose-colored glasses, refusing to acknowledge that their lives are in total chaos. These people may experience their health slowly disintegrating, because their bodies take on the full stress loads that their souls refuse to face. Some soft souls feel responsible for saving everyone and feel anguish over the lack of peace in the world. Others fade away from who they are, become invisible to the world, and fail to fully use their talents and gifts. They may give away their soft souls to become caretakers to those who need them. We see this often in wives and mothers, who lose the persons they were before they became wives and mothers. On other occasions, some soft souls become self-destructive, turning to substances to hide from their losses and pain.

When sober, many addicts are among the most tenderhearted souls. Drugs and alcohol bring out another side of which they are often ashamed. Some soft souls eventually fall into bitterness and anger. They continue patterns of abuse from their families or simply refuse to acknowledge opinions other than their own. They isolate themselves and blame others for their loneliness, and that blame only enflames their bitterness. The ways that soft souls try to protect themselves from the harsh world are numerous, and some soft souls use a combination of these methods.

Hardness fails to protect; bitterness separates us; internalized stress and substances destroy us. So what are we to do? We believe that the solution is to refuse the negative message from the world about our soft souls and to accept our original God-given spirits while also honoring the paths that we have taken and the protections we have given ourselves. All of our protective tendencies are destructive in the extreme, but many can have great value when used properly. And no matter what choices we have made in life, we can't go back in time and change them. So one key is to honor the paths we have taken and learn from them rather than live in shame from our choices. All of your life events and choices have molded you into the beautiful person you are today and need to be embraced, because these are the things that have formed you. We derive our true strengths from both returning to who we were meant to be and embracing the paths and choices we have made to navigate this harsh world. This gives us strength. The strength to change our circumstances, the strength to stand up to the world and make it less harsh, the strength to find a purpose for everything, and the strength to love others when we are not being loved. Healing lies in the integration of our trueness, our original states, our softness, with the ways we have chosen to protect ourselves from a world that might have destroyed us if we had not found ways to protect our tender spirits. When the soft soul embraces his or her true identity and the path he or she has journeyed, strength develops and grows.

So for all of you who watch the news and feel deep pain about the world we live in, for those who are barely holding on to your softness by a prayer, for those who have surrendered to the hardness and found it left you dead inside and continuously dissatisfied, for those who care deeply about someone who is a soft soul, we offer this book. Our words have been written to help you know that you are not alone and to help you adore and recapture/reintegrate your soft soul.

CHAPTER 2

WHAT QUALIFIES SOMEONE AS A SOFT SOUL?

ARE YOU THE TYPE OF PERSON WHO CRIES AT SENTIMENTAL COMMERCIALS? Are you deeply bothered or angered by injustices in the world? Do you care for others easily and with sacrifice? Do you experience great joy in making others happy? Have you been hurt or victimized by the world? Do you seem to feel more deeply than most people? If any of these things are true, you may be a soft soul.

We all have different stories to tell, but we share a common experience; the world has affected us. For some, the impact is significant but not devastating; we just feel deeply and wish many things in this world were different, but we cope well and live good lives. For others, the world has taken the beautiful soft souls we were born with and hurt them, manipulated them, and sometimes even broken them. We struggle to cope, to survive, to overcome, but we are changed nonetheless. Some of us build strong defenses in order to survive (and even thrive), and others live in constant pain or fear. Maybe this describes you, or maybe it describes someone about whom you care deeply. Some of us have always been soft souls, and some of us become more like a soft soul as we experience life. We tend to respond differently to the harsh realities of the world. Some fight the way the world is, while others escape into addiction or hide from the world. These attempts at protection are often temporarily necessary, as our souls are so tender that they cannot stand the losses and hurts that the world will offer to us at times. We see people develop these protective behaviors for a good reason: the pain is just too intense. Unfortunately, while these protective defenses temporarily protect us, when overused, they can consume us and hurt us.

Challenge itself is not a bad thing. A certain amount of difficulty in this world grows us, matures us, and strengthens us. However, a predisposition toward a soft soul combined with intense challenge can create great pain. It is like cooking. If you undercook something, it won't reach its potential of taste; if you overcook it, the dish could be hard to eat or inedible. All of the ingredients are there, and the dish has the potential to be delicious, but the amount of heat affects the final product. That said, this book does not focus on those individuals who have *not* experienced enough heat; rather, it focuses on those who have gone through the fire.

When you have been through intense pain in life, healing your soft soul becomes a balancing act between risking the hurt of the world, which is needed to fully experience the wonderful blessings of the world, and navigating this life in a way that keeps us from unnecessary or damaging hurt. Soft souls who live with no defenses crumble; soft souls who overuse their protective behaviors risk missing out on the joys of the world and, at times, hurting others while they protect themselves. In this chapter, we will explore what types of people are or become soft souls.

What qualifies someone as a truly soft soul? While people may have various degrees of softness, we believe that there are both personality factors and environmental situations that develop individuals into soft souls.

Certain types of personalities will predetermine someone to be a soft soul:

- People who are merciful and forgive easily
- Individuals who have a deep and innate sense of justice and fairness
- Those who yearn for peace and the end of conflict
- People who search for meaning and feel deeply there is something missing from their life (which we will refer to as "poor in spirit")
- Individuals who are meek and gentle by nature

Intense life experiences can create or bring out your soft soul:

- Being victimized and persecuted by others
- Experiencing deep and/or frequent loss in your life

Let's examine each of these in detail, looking at their tendencies and also how each creates a specific vulnerability to the world.

THE MERCIFUL: THOSE WHO FORGIVE EASILY

Many people have great difficulty forgiving those who have hurt them, but not the merciful. These individuals are unusually kind, caring souls who seem incapable of carrying a grudge. They believe in forgiveness instead of revenge, which is a beautiful characteristic. Phrases like "It's OK" or "Of course I forgive you" flow quickly and easily from their lips. They accept the humanness in all of us and understand that people make mistakes. Yes, the merciful are truly lovely soft souls.

While the ability and willingness to forgive is an incredibly admirable quality, showing mercy in the extreme creates a vulnerability to pain. Without proper boundaries, these people put themselves in the position of potentially being hurt over and over in the same way. The merciful often feel constant disappointment because of their belief that all people can (and want to) change and treat people well. Hurting others makes no sense to them, and sometimes, they feel guilty if they create boundaries to protect themselves. Honoring their soft souls means they must forgive, but the merciful benefit from accepting that you can forgive and yet still protect yourself from the abuse of others. For example, a woman who is regularly physically abused by her husband needs to separate from him until he receives treatment (or, many times, permanently). She can still forgive him and not wish him horrible circumstances or want revenge, but she must remove herself from that dangerous situation. Being merciful does not mean being a victim.

THE RIGHTEOUS: THOSE WHO HAVE AN INNATE SENSE OF RIGHT AND WRONG

Have you ever met someone who has an incredible sense of what is fair or just? Such people want the world to be right, for people to be treated fairly, for truth to be spoken, for appropriate consequences to follow negative actions. These individuals are often attracted to jobs in law enforcement where they can have the opportunity to right the wrongs of the world and make sure evildoers pay for the harm they cause others.

Most people desire fairness, but these individuals *demand* in the extreme that the world be fair. Unfortunately, life on this planet is not always fair or just. At times, you see people who do selfish and hurtful things thrive while others who are giving and loving experience great hardships. This creates vulnerability for those who demand justice because, since this world is not always just and fair, they live in a state of frequent or constant frustration. They become angry with the world for the lack of justice and fight battles that often cannot be won. For example, we have seen people whose spouses have been unfaithful go through divorces where most of their net worth went to attorneys because of their desire to teach their spouses a lesson. They are willing to lose much in order to win. In this example, honoring their soft souls means that they need to take a stand for what is right; however, the righteous would benefit from not creating for themselves that additional pain of intense financial loss by accepting that the scales may not be balanced in this situation.

THE PEACEKEEPERS: THOSE WHO WANT HARMONY

Another type of soft soul is the peacekeeper. Peacekeepers have a longing for peace between all people. They despise conflict and desperately want others to live in respectful and loving relationships. "Can't we all just get along?" is their motto. They will do whatever they can to smooth over conflicts and get people to communicate. Their desire for peace is usually both interpersonal and for the world at large. Watching television and seeing a world at war creates great sadness for them.

The peacekeepers' vulnerability comes from their willingness to do whatever it takes to maintain the peace. They will quickly give in, putting their own desires to the side in order to make others happy. Unfortunately, over time, this can make peacekeepers bitter because they feel like they are the only ones willing to sacrifice. Paradoxically, they are hesitant to share their upset for fear of causing a conflict. Honoring their soft souls means that they often want to make others happy, and that is admirable, but peacekeepers benefit from learning that sometimes saying no is the best thing for the other person and for their relationships long-term. For example, the individual who goes overboard at work to help coworkers but ends up feeling like no one helps them may need to say no to the one coworker who tends to depend too much on them. The peacekeeper also has to learn to ask for the help that he or she needs.

THE POOR IN SPIRIT: THOSE WHO SEARCH FOR MEANING AND FEEL DEEPLY THAT SOMETHING IS MISSING

Of all of the types of soft souls, the poor in spirit may be the most difficult to understand. Some people believe the poor in spirit have low self-esteem, and while that may be the case with some, we think poor in spirit goes deeper than that. We will be using "poor in spirit" to describe anyone who feels that this world is not enough or who feels a huge gap between what they are and what they are supposed to be. In a religious sense, it is someone who is deeply troubled by the sins of the world or feels a gap between what God created them to be and what they actually are or do. The poor in spirit have trouble finding happiness because something always seems off or wrong. They feel a hole in their souls, as if they awoke in a world in which they do not belong. The beautiful thing about the poor in spirit is that they have a heightened awareness about things that others are often oblivious to or ignore. They are connected to the potential of what we could be and the sense of something out there that is beyond us.

That said, being poor in spirit creates several vulnerabilities. These vulnerabilities could come in the following forms:

- A nagging feeling of being different and feeling a lack of connection to other people
- A constant sense of disconnection from God (or that God is disappointed in them)
- A deep sadness about how the world actually is much of the time
- A consuming awareness that they are failing to live up to their potential

Honoring their soft souls means embracing their heightened sensitivity/ awareness as an incredible gift and using it as a guide to something better rather than a discontent that leads to judging themselves and others as inadequate. When the poor in spirit can embrace their gifts and use them as compasses versus judgments, they can live wonderful lives of pursuing that potential and the power that exists beyond all of us. They can celebrate the journey. For example, this describes the Christian who can realize that the world is fallen and cruel at times but who, instead of getting depressed by that, dedicates their life to the pursuit of God and caring for others and finds comfort in the grace God offers all.

THE MEEK: THOSE WHO ARE GENTLE AND SOFT-SPOKEN

Some would say that the meek are the softest of souls. They are sensitive, quiet, or shy people who speak softly with kindness and humility. They avoid the spotlight and prefer to be in the background, quietly supporting and caring for others. A myriad of words could describe these individuals: humble, timid, submissive, docile, modest, compliant, and mild. The beauty of the meek is that they would not hurt a fly; they are gentle lambs. Unfortunately, these lambs are often the prey for the wolves of the world.

The meek are by nature quite vulnerable to others, and many take advantage of them. Because of their submissive natures, they may forgo their own compasses to follow someone else's direction. Their timidity is sometimes a magnet for the arrogant, the overbearing, and the controlling. The beauty of their easygoing natures can be selfishly abused by those who take pleasure in overpowering others. This leaves them to often being hurt by those who manipulate their softness. The shadow side of their humility is a lack of trust in their own strength and decision-making ability that leads them to following others with stronger and more assertive personalities. While many relationships can healthily exist with one person more assertive than the other, if the person with the stronger personality is unhealthy, this could lead the meek to many roads of destruction, including simply living to serve someone else or, at extremes, some forms of addiction if they fall in with the wrong people. Honoring their soft souls means embracing their humility and softer approach while also learning to trust their opinions, feelings, and beliefs and to be willing to stand up for these. For example, the person at work who rarely speaks up at team meetings could have a huge positive impact by, on occasion, speaking assertively and taking a stand on an issue of importance to them.

THE VICTIMS: THOSE WHO HAVE BEEN SEVERELY HURT OR PERSECUTED

The previous types of soft souls were based on personality. The next two are based on life experiences. The first type is people who have been severely victimized by others. This could range from anyone who has been physically, sexually, or emotionally abused to anyone who has been completely abandoned or neglected by parents or others around them. While at times the vulnerability to being victimized can be related to another type of soft soul (such as the merciful or meek), at other times, it is simply related to who has been in their lives. Perhaps they had a parent with mental illness who abused them physically, emotionally, or sexually. Perhaps they married someone who was narcissistic or controlling and used them for their own selfish desires. Perhaps someone married a soft soul for money and left when they met someone else. Sadly, the list of the ways human beings can victimize each other is quite extensive.

So what vulnerabilities come with being victimized? If experienced enough, it can create bitterness and a lack of trust in others. Also, especially if soft souls were victimized early in life, they might start seeing themselves as victims. Many times, therapy can accidentally reinforce this identity by focusing on the fact that there was nothing these patients could do and allowing them to continue to talk about the pains they have experienced in life. Paradoxically and sadly, this can create the victim identity, which in turn creates danger. What happens to victims? They get victimized! So seeing themselves as victims can, at times, increase their likelihood of future victimization. That said, victims must vent and grieve the terrible wrongdoings that they have experienced; they just need to work at the same time to take full responsibility for their current and future lives. For example, a person who was sexually abused by a relative must confront that abuse (and many times the relative) and grieve the pain experienced. At the same time, they must also refuse to let that event or series of events define who they are and work to live a happy and fulfilling life.

THE MOURNERS: THOSE WHO GO THROUGH DEEP AND/OR FREQUENT LOSS

The pain victims experience comes from other people. The hurt that mourners experience is more likely to result from the fact that life can often be unforgiving or random. Again, the list is sadly extensive: the parents who lose a child at birth or early in life, the husband who loses his wife to cancer despite her obsession with healthy living, the wife who loses her husband to a heart attack even though he was an avid runner. Any of us are vulnerable to these occurrences that many times seem to have no rhyme or reason. Most of us do relatively well with *expected* loss, like losing your ninety-year-old grandmother. You miss her terribly, but you accept her death as a part of life. It is much more difficult when the loss does not match what we believe life or God was going to offer us.

Massive hurt creates a vulnerability to the loss of hope, and few things are more devastating than losing hope. Many mourners try to protect themselves from future disappointment by discarding hope and always expecting the worst thing to happen. This can create a deep depression. Hope is a powerful force that can energize and focus us. Hope for good things happening in our lives can lead us to take actions that can increase the odds that we will be blessed with good things. For example, a parent who grieves the loss of a child but lives in the hope that they will see them again in heaven, a spouse who grieves the loss of a partner but is able to find love again without guilt, anyone willing to pick themselves up to try and try again.

• • •

We have discussed personality factors related to being a soft soul, such as being merciful, righteous, a peacekeeper, poor in spirit, and meek. We also discussed life experiences, such as being victimized and persecuted by others or experiencing deep loss from life events. If we have experienced a harsh environment, we must come up with ways to protect ourselves, or we could crumble from our experiences. The next section of this book will cover each type of soft soul while also addressing six archetypal ways that people try to protect themselves from this tough world, mainly told through the story of a family (our family) of soft souls.

The Greek roots of the word *archetype* are *archein* and *typos*, which mean "original or old" and "pattern, model, or type," respectively. Many psychologists and researchers have studied archetypes, including famous psychologist Carl Jung. Some focus on common patterns found in literature and mythology, while others (including your authors) focus primarily on universal or common patterns of human behavior. Many variations of archetypes are promoted in different theories. We have chosen to focus on six common archetypes or common characteristics/patterns of behavior that we feel are specific to soft souls and are used to protect from the difficulties and challenges of the world. Each archetype has its own motivation, set of values, and personality characteristics.

The six methods of protection that we will focus on through our stories are:

1. The Idealist, who soothes and protects by ignoring the negative and believing it will get better.

2. The Charmer, who soothes by getting attention and "love" from others.

3. The Fighter, who protects by getting angry instead of getting hurt.

4. The Pleaser, who soothes by making everyone happy so the world doesn't feel so bad.

5. The Invisible One, who becomes unseen in order to avoid the pains of the world.

6. The Addicted One, who soothes by medicating the pain.

We have attached different types of soft souls with each individual's story and protective style. For example, the Idealist is connected to the soft soul quality of being merciful; the Invisible One is connected to being poor in spirit; the Addicted One is connected to being meek. That said, any type of soft soul could develop any of these protective approaches (even several at the same time). Being meek could lead to protecting yourself with invisibility, addiction, idealism, etc. While some types of soft souls naturally gravitate to certain protections (like peacekeepers who become pleasers), no one protection method fits each type of soft soul. In fact, you may see yourself using several of these protection strategies. While we will only cover six archetypes in this book, there are many additional ways that people try to protect themselves. Some examples are:

- The Thinker, who tries to protect by shutting off their emotions.

- The Jester, who tries to protect by joking and distracting from the pain.

- The Caregiver, who protects by focusing away from their own circumstances and emotions and instead on the needs of others.

- The Artist, who escapes into a world of imagination and dreams to avoid the pains of the world.

- The Rebel, who tries to protect by being different and breaking the rules.

- The Ruler, who craves power and authority as a way to protect him- or herself.

- The Zealot, who tries to protect through superiority generated from extreme religiosity or obsessive focus on a cause.

So there are many ways that we try to navigate this harsh world, and you can learn more about these other archetypes on our website, softsouls.com. With this book, we will be focusing on six.

We now invite you into our lives as you read about the journey to adapt to the world while still maintaining your soft soul.

PART TWO

LIVING IN A HARSH WORLD

....

CHAPTER 3

SOFT SOULS
WHO ARE MERCIFUL

The Story of an Idealist

THE IDEALIST

....

Merciful. It was the word her family would most often use when describing Frances. She had mercy for the little girl in the neighborhood who all of the other children made fun of, mercy for the old people who had no one to love them, and mercy and forgiveness for people in her life who did not always deserve that mercy. It was hard for Frances to understand how people could be cruel to others, why people would purposely hurt others, and how people could ignore others who were clearly in need. She didn't understand it, but she would forgive it and always hope that people would change.

THE IDEALIST'S BEGINNINGS

Frances was the baby of the family, an adorable tot with a love of music and a dreamy disposition. She adored her mother and, throughout her childhood, often spent hours in the kitchen just watching her mother work while talking about whatever was on her young mind. There were six children. They were a singing family like the Von Trapps, but their life was not *The Sound of Music*. Her father (despite the fact that he could barely carry a tune) was the captain of the family choir. She remembered how he picked apart their performance after every show. Frances didn't realize her incredible talent because she felt that, in her father's eyes, it was never good enough. She shuddered as she heard the sound of his voice singing in the living room. She sat next to her mother on the organ bench and watched as he strained his voice to hit the notes. Every sour note from her father had a repercussion for Frances's mother. She hadn't "hit the note right," she hadn't "played fast enough," she hadn't "held the note," her father would complain. Frances knew her mother was a talented pianist and yet was constantly subjected to these unfair critiques.

On one such occasion when she was around five years old, Frances looked up from her chair and, without thinking, opened her mouth and said, "Can't you do anything but fight?" She shocked herself as it slipped out and quickly backed away as she saw her father coming toward her. He grabbed her by the wrist, and she felt her body painfully spin like a top as it slid across the wooden floor. Frances landed under the organ and lay dazed for a minute. Then she got angry. As the tears burned her eyes, she pulled herself up and ran, furious, not about being hurt but that her little body had not broken the organ so that her father would have to pay to have it repaired.

Frances's father did many things to her that most people would struggle to forgive, but Frances always forgave him. However, she knew this was not the kind of man she would eventually marry. In her mind, she dreamed of a different life, a life full of love, children, and serving God.

THE IDEALIST'S BROTHER

Frances's oldest brother was her idol; he was the man she wished her father could be. While her father was often cold, cruel, and abusive in her eyes, her brother was kind and caring. Since Frances was too small to defend herself or her mother, her brother was the only protection they had.

Frances's mother was the sweetest soul who had ever lived. She was beautiful, so full of grace, with a childlike grin. When her husband was not home, she often giggled like a little girl full of joy and freedom. Frances loved it when her mother's laughter filled their home. Her mother rarely laughed when Frances's father was home and placated him in order to keep him happy. His tirades terrified Frances as a little girl, but her mother held that sweet smile as often as she could, as if to tell her children, "I am OK; everything will be fine." Frances's mother carried herself with a tender, silent peace that made everyone around her feel at ease. How could anyone harm a woman like that?

However, their father did, and on one particular day, he slapped their mother in front of them. That was the last straw; it finally became too much for Frances's oldest brother to bear. Barely sixteen, he had watched his mother be mistreated one too many times, so he leaped up and positioned his body offensively between his mother and father. An all-too-familiar rage filled his father's eyes, but he did not care; he had drawn the line, and there was no backing down. "If you ever hit her again, I'm going to teach you a lesson," he boldly declared. His mother tried to silence him, afraid of what her husband would do. Frances could not believe it as her father backed down from the physical confrontation that he knew he could never win. Staring coldly at his oldest son, he commanded him out of his home and told him he was not to return. At first, their mother pleaded for her oldest child, but her husband had that wild look in his eyes, and she knew that she did not dare cross him for her children's sake. So she became silent as her son left the house.

Frances's heart broke for her big brother. She was so afraid without him home. She wondered how he was getting along. Was he lonely at the YMCA that took him in? Was he ever coming back? Their mother snuck him food and money, risking her husband's wrath. Frances feared for her mother. Eventually, her brother was allowed back, but Frances found forgiveness far more difficult after that day.

THE IDEALIST GOES TO COLLEGE

As Frances grew up, she continued to be interested in music and ministry and decided to attend a college that could equip her to serve God. She hoped that Bible college would provide her that ideal life, and she worked very hard to get there. She sang with girlfriends at a local department store and various functions to raise money for college. She took care of her oldest sister's young son for the summer before leaving. During this time, she watched as her sister dealt with a husband who was cold and cheating. It made her even more determined to meet her goal of an ideal marriage and life. She was going to Bible college to pursue her music and to make sure she found a husband who loved God as much as she did. While it was difficult to leave for college, Frances was comforted with the knowledge that she would soon be coming home at the first college break.

Being at school was liberating, and Frances loved her first semester. She almost hated to return home for break, but she missed her sweet mother so much. Frances waited at the bus stop, anxiously looking for her father's car to come around the bend and take her home for a visit. It was one of the few times she was anxious to see him, because it meant she was one step closer to hugging her mother. His car came around the bend. Frances's heart leaped as she saw the other person in the car. She wouldn't have to wait. Her mother had come to pick her up too. The car came closer, and she froze as she realized the woman in the car was not her mother. Frances's father gave no explanation. He actually sat her between himself and the woman. They dropped the woman off in silence, and he said nothing until they pulled up to their home. "Don't say anything to your mother. She wouldn't understand, and it would upset her."

Frances said nothing. She held everything inside, and her mother sensed her daughter's uneasiness. As they sat at the dinner table, the phone rang. Her mother rose from the table and came back with the phone. "Phyllis is on the phone," she said.

Frances's father jumped up from the table, shouting at his youngest daughter. "I can't believe my baby betrayed me. I can't believe you told." His wife looked at him, stunned. Frances had said nothing. She had kept her father's secret, but he had just given it away. Frances returned to college vowing that her husband would be different. Her spouse would be kind and faithful. She would lead an ideal life with a good man.

THE IDEALIST MEETS THE CHARMER

In her sophomore year on the campus of her Bible college in the hills of Tennessee, Frances began to notice a cocky boy named Ken with a charming smile and a funny wit. It took two weeks for the boy to muster the courage to tell Frances that he had broken up with his girlfriend. He had always come across as confident, but it was an act he had perfected from a childhood filled with rejection. Finally, one day, Ken walked through campus with Frances. "So how would a young man in Ohio ask a young girl out?" he hinted, hiding his nervousness. Frances smiled coyly. "The same way they would do it in Indiana." Her smile made Ken feel desired in a way he never had before. The cocky confidence he portrayed on the outside seemed to seep inside him. She made him feel worthy.

When they started dating, Frances had no idea about the rejection this boy had experienced all of his life. All she knew was that Ken was athletic, admired by his classmates, and could preach like no one she had ever heard. He was the opposite of her father, with his dark hair, dark eyes, and comical sense of humor. It did not take long to love him. It did not take long until she believed he was the answer to her prayers. She was completely content.

They seemed like a well-matched couple—both attractive, incredibly talented, and with a deep desire to turn their lives over to God's will. Frances was the musical one, with a beautiful voice that inspired people wherever she went. Ken couldn't sing a note and would spend much of his life as the butt of music jokes, but he could speak. When Ken preached, it was as if God came and sat beside you right there in the pew, telling you how much He loved you, telling you how He expected your all, telling you where you had made Him proud and where you needed to change. Yes, Ken could preach. It was truly his God-given gift, and Frances believed that together they would bring many to know and love the Lord.

THE DREAM

One night, Frances had a horrible dream that she had been killed in an accident. The next morning, she cried on Ken's shoulder. Something about the dream was haunting her. She was about to leave for fall break, and despite knowing that it was only a dream, Frances feared that she would never see Ken again.

When fall break came to an end, Ken received a message; it said Frances had been killed in an accident. Ken's knees went out from under him. He was shattered. He tried to call her parents, but no one answered. His mind swirling, Ken called the school and sobbed when he heard a familiar voice answer the phone. It was Frances. She was alive, but her voice was shaking and weak. The message had been a mistake. She was fine, but her sweet brother—her idol, her strength—had been in an accident. His vehicle had crashed on a bridge. He was gone.

Frances wondered if her father thought about the day he had thrown his son out as they carried his coffin to the graveside. Her mother's heart had hurt so much, being separated from her oldest child just for those few weeks. How would she now live without him forever? Frances trembled as she watched her mother's face, the devastated face of a mother who had lost a child. She knew her own deep and intense pain but could only imagine the depths of her mother's mourning.

THE IDEALIST MEETS THE CHARMER'S NOT-SO-CHARMING MOTHER

Frances was so nervous. She and Ken had only been dating a few weeks, but she already had such strong feelings for him that meeting his parents was a big deal. Ken's father was a handsome man, large and strong from working in the steel mills all of his life. Even though he had adopted Ken, there was a similarity in their looks. Ken's father had kind eyes, a scruffy unshaven face, and a welcoming smile, but he said very little. Ken's father loved his wife; that was obvious. He doted on her every need. In fact, it seemed like both men doted on her.

Ken's mother was bigger boned than the women in Frances's family, which made her a little intimidating, but she was still quite lovely. Her auburn hair starkly contrasted with her beautiful blue eyes. Her tan skin seemed slightly more worn than it should be for a woman her age, perhaps the side effect of her heavy smoking habit. She spoke with a long drawl from her years of living in the Kentucky hills. She was not a dumb woman, but her lack of education showed in her choice of words. There was also an apparent jealousy of Frances. She did not like her son looking to another woman for approval.

Ken's mother behaved herself through the evening, and he thought things had gone well. Right before they left, his mother took Frances aside and, with angry eyes and a stern tone, informed her, "We have paid a lot of money for our son's education, so you better not screw it up." It was clear to Frances that nobody dared mess with this woman. Despite Ken's mother's aggression, Frances knew it would all work out.

THE ENGAGEMENT

Frances believed that love could conquer anything and that life was going to be beautiful. The announcement of her engagement to Ken was readily accepted by her family, and while Frances's mother had expressed some concerns over the young pastor's ego, she also saw Ken's kinder side and knew that her daughter loved him.

Ken's mother did not handle the news as well. Frances had done nothing to her, and yet Ken's mother seemed to hate her. Perhaps it was because they were so different from each other. Frances was sweet, gentle, and always seemed to see the positive in others, while Ken's mother was tough and often negative. On the other hand, perhaps she was simply jealous that her son gave all of his attention to Frances. For whatever reason, she took pleasure in torturing Frances, even refusing to refer to her by name. She called her simply "that girl."

On Frances's first visit, Ken's mother had mocked the young girl for a few burned kernels of popcorn she had cooked. Frances cried at the criticism, which only fueled the mother's delighted tormenting. "*That girl is so emotional,*" she would often cackle as this pattern kept emerging. It infuriated Ken's mother to see her son rush to his girlfriend's side to try to comfort her. "She's just manipulating you!" She made it clear that she would rather her son marry anyone else, even a woman of another race, which in her horribly racist mind was the worst thing he could have done until Frances came along.

Nevertheless, Frances tried to please Ken's mother. She felt God would want her to honor her for Ken's sake and, being an idealist, believed that she would eventually come around. As her relationship with Ken blossomed, his mother became increasingly jealous and verbally abusive. Frances did not go with Ken when he announced their engagement to his family. She did not want to be subjected to his mother's predictable, hateful reaction. When they finally saw each other again, Ken's mother looked at Frances with disdain and, drawing on her cigarette, said, "A thousand souls will burn in hell because of you marrying my son!"

Frances's gentle soul shriveled at her remarks. This was the worst thing she could have said. Frances and Ken's life purpose was bringing souls to God. It was the final straw for Ken. His rage took over. He would not allow his mother to do this to the woman he loved. "If you continue to hurt my fiancée, you will never see me again." Strangely, despite the fact that his mother had often treated him with such disdain, the idea that her son would walk away from her for this simpering little girl was unimaginable. She shut her mouth and, for a time, was silent.

THE FIRST BETRAYAL

Back at college, Frances was crying when Ken came to her, and his savior mode clicked in. He hurried to her side, wanting to ease her pain, to save the day. As she looked up at him, he saw a horrible sorrow, but there was something else. He saw in her a look he knew too well. Somehow, he had disappointed her. Frances cried as she told Ken that she had heard a rumor that he had kissed another girl. At first, he wanted to lie, but he looked around him at the campus of his Bible college. He could not lie here. This was his new life. He would not be the fallen boy of his past. Ken admitted his failure to Frances. It had been a brief kiss with a female friend as they were saying good-bye, but it turned into something more passionate. He was truly, truly sorry. Ken waited for Frances's response. He wanted her forgiveness so badly. The silence tormented him.

"I forgive you," Frances said, finally looking at him. Her words spoke exoneration, but her eyes still carried the disappointment. He had failed her, and that knowledge cut him deeply. It would have been easier had she been mad at him. Ken could have dealt with that, but that look in her eyes made him feel a familiar sense of failure and worthlessness, and instead of being grateful, he found himself resenting Frances.

THE MARRIAGE OF THE IDEALIST AND THE CHARMER

"I will never marry a man like my father." It was Frances's life mantra. She vowed to marry a kind man, and while Ken's mother had talked of his temper, Frances had never seen it. She had vowed to marry a faithful man. Given how guilty Ken felt about the kiss with his friend, Frances believed he would never cheat on her. He loved her too much; he loved God too much. Frances's marriage would be different, and she and her husband would spend their entire lives devoted to each other. She believed it with all her heart. She was, after all, an Idealist.

The church was beautiful and the bride even more beautiful. Frances was petite, and through her veil, Ken could see her beautiful brown eyes. On this day, those eyes were full of hope and ideals. Ken stood at the front waiting for her to be with him, to be his forever. Frances had loved him as he had never been loved. She had forgiven him his faults and, on this day, had set all doubts aside. Once they were together as man and wife, her new husband would be satisfied and have no need to look at other women. Frances knew that their life could be perfect. She looked at Ken's eyes, so full of love and pride, and she was proud to be his. He was a man who could move people, whom God loved and had chosen just like King David in the Bible, and they had a destiny.

"Wither thou goest, I will go." She spoke from her heart the Bible verse that meant so much. "And where thou lodgest, I will lodge: thy people shall be my people, and thy God my God."

A cry rang out and echoed through the church. It became more dramatic as Frances spoke. It was her soon-to-be mother-in-law, hysterically sobbing, "My baby's getting married." Ken looked away from his mother and smiled at his bride. She was everything his mother had never been to him.

Frances continued. "Where thou diest, will I die, and there will I be buried: the Lord do so to me, and more also, if ought but death part thee and me."

The ceremony concluded, and Frances and Ken were ready to start their lives together. They were both young and excited about the future that they would share together forever.

CHAPTER 4

....

ARE YOU AN IDEALIST?

So how have you adapted to the brutal effects of this harsh world on your soft soul? We will look at these common adaptation/protection strategies in each of our chapters between the stories of this family of soft souls. For each type of adaptation, we will give a general overview, review its main tendencies, state what is positive about each, explore the shadow side of each, and then give specific recommendations if you are overusing that type of protection.

Please note that when it comes to ways of protecting yourself, one size does not necessarily fit all, but some sizes do fit many people. You may see parts of several types of protection strategies in yourself. Also, we want to be very careful about giving a negative label to the shadow sides of the soft soul's gifts. For some soft souls, these shadow sides are more pronounced than for others. We simply present these as tendencies to consider. We also want to make it clear that the soft soul family we discussed in this book does not necessarily show every one of these tendencies.

Another thing to note is that some parts of this book will be spiritual or religious in nature. This was the cause of much discussion between the authors. On one hand, we do not want to preach at anyone. We grew up being preached at and do not find it particularly healthy at times. On the other hand, we didn't want to ignore that spirituality is, in our minds, core to navigating life as a soft soul. So our compromise is to share what we believe and feel in as genuine a way as possible while hopefully communicating our respect for different beliefs (even the authors do not have identical beliefs). We believe that much harm has been caused in the world by individuals using religion for power or dominance. That is not our intent. Our intent is to share our belief that our Creator made us to be divinely His, and He can help us become the people we are supposed to be. We offer these suggestions to simply share what we have found works in our lives. Your relationship with God may be different than ours. That is the grand mystery of God, and we believe that your personal journey to understand truth and our Creator can take lots of twists, turns, and different perspectives. With that said, let's look at the idealistic soft soul.

UNDERSTANDING THE IDEALIST

The idealistic soft soul is full of optimism and hope. These individuals see the best in every situation, trust unconditionally, and always expect things to work out for the good of everyone. Idealists can be a joy to be around. They smile often and have a refreshing outlook on life. Idealists give mercy and forgiveness to others very quickly and often expect that unconditional love and acceptance will heal people of almost any wound or temptation. If you have ever been around a pessimist for any period of time, you realize what a blessing it is to be close to an Idealist. This type of soft soul is a beacon of light in a world that can be so dark. Other descriptions that have been used to describe the Idealist include the innocent, the saint, and the dreamer.

While idealism is a powerful positive force, this tendency often does not protect the Idealist from the harshness of the world. Even though giving people the benefit of the doubt is a wonderful and beautiful tendency, it can also result in gullibility and lack of discernment. Idealists are often surprised when others do not show the same type of loyalty, trust, love, service, and care that they show automatically. Thus their soft souls, if not protected, can be deceived and betrayed by those who do not share their same level of powerful and dedicated love.

Major Tendencies

Idealists see the best in everything. They are optimistic by nature and love to dream of great accomplishments or the perfect life. Despite having soft souls, Idealists can weather many storms in life because of a never-dying hope that tomorrow will be better. Idealists are full of mercy for other people. They long for paradise and happiness. Idealists want to do things right and be kind to all.

The Positive Aspects

Always hopeful, rarely defeated, Idealists have the uncanny ability to see all the good in people and in life. They have resilient spirits and can be great encouragers to others. Idealists forgive easily. They are usually full of faith and optimism.

The Shadow Side

The potential shadow side of Idealists is that they can be viewed as not fully understanding others' challenges and as naive in their view of the world. Their words of encouragement could be seen by others as placating or not addressing the core of the other person's challenge. Another shadow side of the Idealists' optimism is that sometimes they trust in situations where trust is not warranted, and they can be taken advantage of by another person. At times, they can be too kind when instead they need to set appropriate boundaries or love someone well enough to speak the truth, even if they find it painful. If not careful, Idealists can become doormats.

Strategies for Integrating Your Soft Soul
While Honoring Your Idealistic Tendencies

- If you are an Idealist, learn to be skeptical. Skepticism is not a negative thing—it is simply the healthy delay of judgment (while pessimism is a predetermined negative outcome). Learn to look at both the potential positive and the negative of a situation so that you will not be blindsided and have your dreams crushed.

- If your dreams have been destroyed, mourn by fully facing the loss. Idealists often avoid mourning in an attempt to stay positive, resulting in the painful memories lingering in their subconscious and affecting future interactions with people. Idealists must mourn fully so they can then focus on creating new dreams that are obtainable and possible.

- When someone is sharing their difficulties with you, focus on empathizing with them and then eventually help them solve their situation and focus on what they can control. Simple responses like "It will all work out" or "If you just pray, it will be fine" are unlikely to be a true comfort to the other person. They need to know that you see the challenges they face and may mistake your optimism for a lack of care.

- Know that forgiving someone is not the same as saying what they did was OK. You have the right to protect yourself from further harm while still being able to forgive and love the person.

- Learn to draw boundaries with other people. You can love people deeply and still put boundaries and rules into place to protect yourself from dysfunctional and harmful behaviors. For example, if you are visiting family and aggressive arguments or attacks come your way, you can set the boundary that you would love to visit those family members as long as everyone acts respectfully. Inform family that if they become aggressive, you will still love them, but you will leave the event quietly to protect yourself.

CHAPTER 5

SOFT SOULS WHO ARE PERSECUTED

The Story of a Charmer

THE CHARMER

Nothing felt as powerful as standing in front of a congregation and sharing the words of God, directing them in the right way to live. Ken was proud that he and his beautiful bride were living God's good life now. He and his young bride helped people, taught people, were there when people welcomed their children into the world, and were there to help people leave this world and go on to heaven. They were saving people from hell, and he felt like he was saved from hell now.

For the most part, Ken was greatly loved by his congregations, but in every church, there were negative people—and women who claimed to be the most godly but who would find fault with everything and everyone. Ken was already so wounded from his past that he could not bear the attacks.

His soft soul carried every persecution as a personal sign of his failure. He needed help, but he was the one others came to for help. He felt there was nowhere for him to go. No one he could trust. His soft soul felt lonely and vulnerable, but church members wanted their pastor to be perfect. Where could he turn for comfort, help, and sanctuary?

THE CHARMER'S BEGINNINGS

Ken's mother had been told that the substance could cause an abortion, and her hand gripped the counter as she tried to make herself swallow the last of the quinine. *This is going to work. This has to work*, she thought. Her throat burned, but she tightened it, forcing the poison down. She wondered how long she would have to keep it there until it did its job, until it rid her of this seed planted in her by the man who had failed her so much. She didn't want another of his children. She didn't want anything more of him inside of her. This baby meant nothing to her. She held in the quinine, hoping to end the life of the son she was yet to know.

No one knows if tears ran down her cheeks after involuntarily throwing up the poison. It had failed. She was going to have this baby. She was going to carry this burden. She was going to watch this child grow up knowing that she had tried to kill him and failed.

A LIFE LESSON

Shattered glass flew everywhere. Ken's friends scattered like frightened little mice between the nearby houses. He started to sprint too. He was a track runner; he could easily have escaped, but he stopped. Gasping for air (more from fear than from exhaustion), he turned and walked back. Ken, not even a teen yet, stood his ground in the slivers of the broken window around his feet.

"Did you break my window?" the owner shouted, running out his door. "Tell the truth!"

Lying would have been so easy. No one other than his scattered friends had seen him hit the baseball. No one could prove it was him. "Yes, sir. I broke it." Ken confessed with lowered eyes. "I'm really sorry. It was an accident."

The man looked at the young boy who trembled, embarrassed and afraid, and the anger faded from his face. "Well, it's good you told the truth. I am going to call your parents to arrange payment for the window, but I'll give you time to tell them first."

"Thank you, sir," the boy said respectfully. His heart felt like it would pound through his shirt, and he said nothing else.

His thoughts raced as he walked the path to his home. How could he have been so stupid as to hit the ball right into that man's window? How dare his friends run off and abandon him! Moreover, how was his mother going to react? Ken almost laughed aloud at his last question. He knew how she would react to his mistake. Ken tried so hard to do the right thing, to make her proud. She wanted him to be something amazing, and yet, despite all of his efforts to this point, he had not achieved that in her eyes. In front of friends and family, she would brag about him. Her son was the brightest, the most moral, better than the rest. However, in their home, she always admonished him for being a disappointment.

It was this confusing pattern of public praise followed by private chastisement that built in Ken a deep-rooted and tormenting self-doubt.

That self-doubt led to a rage stemming from her rejection and then a fear of what he could do if his rage ever became uncontrollable. He felt guilty for even feeling it, but the older he got, the more his emotions steered his fate. It was a pattern Ken would find impossible to break for most of his life.

His mother's voice was in Ken's head as he took the final steps toward his house. She would say it again, as she had done before—he was a bad seed, bad like his father. He would rather she say anything, that she beat him or turn her back, but no, she always used those piercing words.

Ken didn't even remember his real father, didn't know what evil he had done. He had died in prison when Ken was just five. He only knew that being compared to him was like being compared to the devil himself in his mother's eyes. As Ken walked, he tried to calm himself by repeating the Lord's Prayer: "Lead us not into temptation but deliver us from evil." At least God would be pleased with him for doing what was right, even if his mother was not. He wanted to please his Creator. God was in the deepest places of his soul even as a child. Pleasing Him meant everything to Ken.

Ken held out hope for the man who had adopted him, the man who had been the father every boy dreamed of, that he would understand. He would be proud of his boy. His son had chosen to stand when others had run away. Ken had shown that he was a man and not a frightened little boy.

As Ken opened the door to their humble home, his head hung down, and with his small voice trembling, he confessed his transgression. He looked up at his adopted father's kind eyes for understanding but saw what he feared most. His father was not proud; he was worried and upset. "Where do you think we are going to get that kind of money? We don't have it!" His father shook his head, sighed, and looked away from his son.

The boy's eyes welled up. "I'm sorry. I am so sorry," he whispered and tried to hide his tears. He wasn't going to cry in front of his father. Ken hated being so soft. Men were not supposed to be soft. Ashamed, he went to his room, wishing he had never been born, never realizing the miracle that God had performed to keep him alive. Not knowing how his mother vomited out the poison before it could destroy him. Not realizing that God had laid out a destiny for him.

Ken heard his mother's hand on the doorknob, and his heart sank as she stepped into his room. She looked down at him lying on his bed. "I don't know what my husband expects; you're just like your father."

In a rage, Ken slammed the door behind her as she turned to leave. The rage filled every nerve and fiber, and he grabbed the chair in his room and tossed it against the wall. He could hear her outside the door talking about him. Ken wanted to cause her the pain she caused him, but he couldn't. She was his mother, and despite everything, he loved her.

Lying in the darkness of his room that night, he tried to ask God to forgive him for his behavior, tried to ask God to help him forgive her. His mind was as dark as the shadowless walls, and confusion kept the words from coming. Instead, he cried. Had he done the wrong thing by being honest? Had his honesty put his family in a terrible position they could not afford? Should he have run away or lied? The Bible said lying was a sin. His mind struggled with the moral dilemma, and he could not sleep. In the end, the message from his parents had been clear. Sometimes, it is better to tell a lie or run from the truth than pay the price of your mistakes. It was a lesson that would stick with Ken for the rest of his life.

MAKING MAMA PROUD

Church was important to Ken's mother. Though neither she nor his stepfather went, their children were not to miss a single Sunday. In her mind, having her children in church somehow raised the entire family to a higher class of people. Born in the hills of Kentucky, her family had been very poor, and she bore the shame of poverty. Perhaps it was that shame that made her so rigid. She hated poverty so much that at the young age of fifteen, she left her family and followed her big sister to the bustling city of Indianapolis to create a new life for herself. Her only hope to escape her miserable life was to find a good man with a stable career and get him to marry her.

She had briefly married another man, but it didn't last, and then she met Ken's father. He had been her hope for a new life, but with difficult financial times, this man of her dreams changed. He became a thief and was incarcerated, leaving her a single parent, struggling to survive. Another person might have said that he did what he had to do to take care of his family in tough times, but Ken's mother saw him as evil and despised him for abandoning her.

Ken felt his mother blamed her children (him especially) for the things she had done to survive those years. Had they not been around, some man would surely have married her. She had strong, high cheekbones, a lovely face, beautiful grayish-blue eyes, and auburn hair. She had a contagious laugh. She would have been a good catch.

GOOD OR EVIL

As he grew into his teen years, Ken would look in the mirror and try to remember his father. He would try to find his father in his own face. He knew he had his biological father's dark hair, although his own spiky hairstyle was a statement of his coolness. His skin coloring, he got from his mother. What part of him was not part of her? Was his father skinny as he was? Was he handsome? Did he have his smile? Did he have his father's dark eyes? Did his father's evil ways live inside him?

The guilt Ken's mother placed on him would have swallowed him up had it not been for his older sister. She was stronger than Ken. She wasn't afraid to stand up for herself. She wasn't quite as soft as he was. She did not allow her mother to blame her, but she could not help her little brother fully accept that it was their mother's issue, not theirs. Ken, however, had a tender, soft soul that absorbed the blow. No one had a clue that these deeply repressed feelings would lead to a love/hate relationship with women throughout his life.

The ability to charm and be admired by women became Ken's respite from nagging self-doubt. He would pursue their attention both emotionally and physically to make up for the emotional hole left in him. *If they love me, if they want me, perhaps I am lovable. Perhaps I am good*, floated deep in his psyche. This false concept led him to pursue young women with desperateness. No amount of attention seemed to be enough to calm Ken's fears of being unwanted and unlovable.

Ken wanted to be godly. He wanted to be heroic. He loved the old serial movies: *The Lone Ranger*, *Flash Gordon*, and *Superman*. The good guys always knew what to do, and they always got the girl. Yes, he was going to be one of the good guys, loved and admired by all women. Maybe then, his mother would be proud; maybe then, she would see him as the man he could be rather than his father's reflection in him. But despite his efforts growing up, he never received this unconditional love for which he was yearning.

THE DECISION

Nearing the end of high school, Ken had been praying daily for God's direction in his life. He was nervous but could not wait to tell his parents where his prayers had led him. He had so desperately longed for his mother's approval all his life. As Ken spoke, he watched her hard face intently. The corners of her beautiful blue eyes raised, and her lips lifted into a proud, full grin. An audible sigh escaped him, as if he had been holding his breath for eighteen years, waiting for his mother to find him worthy. Ken had finally done it; he had finally risen above her condemnation, no longer defined as the child of a man she despised, no longer the unwanted baby that she had been so desperate to be rid of. Her baby was going to be a preacher.

This decision to become a pastor led Ken to leave home for Bible college, where he met and eventually married Frances.

AN IDEAL LIFE

Once Frances and Ken were married, they were ready to embark on their mission to serve God. They bought their first house, and though it wasn't much, it was their home. Frances didn't complain about its size or its age. She seemed happy to be with the man she loved. She did hint, however, that she hated the big, red flowers on the wall of their bedroom.

The young preacher was happy to show his wife how handy he could be. He bought paint and set out to make his wife the room of her dreams. But he couldn't get the white paint to cover those big, red flowers. He painted coat after coat, and with each coat of paint, he grew angrier. Ken tried to fight back the rage.

His wife sensed he was upset. Frances reached out a gentle and loving hand to touch him. Ken didn't want her sympathy. He was supposed to be her charmer; he was supposed to be the one fixing things; he was supposed to receive her admiration and praise.

Frances's hand touched Ken's cheek, and before he knew what he was doing, Ken grabbed her arms and forced them behind her back until her elbows met. He screamed at her and then stepped back.

Ken couldn't believe what he had done. His wife cried. Frances was devastated and angry. Ken felt ashamed. He feared he would lose her, and she was the best thing in his life. He repented, sobbing almost uncontrollably, and asked for her mercy.

Frances had a gift for forgiveness, and she lovingly forgave her tortured husband. She could tell his behavior had broken him. Surely, this was an isolated thing, and he would never repeat it.

THE IDEALIST AND THE CHARMER HAVE A SON

Their boy looked so cute wrapped in the baby blanket. His big eyes were so beautiful, so deep. Ken smiled at his firstborn child with pride. He would be a wonderful father, as his adoptive father had been to him. He would not let his son down as his biological father had let him down. His son would learn from him how to be a better man, how to love God and do good things in this world.

For two years, they seemed so happy. Frances was a natural mother; she loved her little boy very much. Her love was so intense that, at times, Ken was almost jealous that his son experienced the motherly love that he yearned for from his own mother. However, he adored being a father. He proudly showed off his little man. Ken was affectionate and loving and would hug his son and tell him how much he loved him. He was so grateful that God had given him this incredible gift.

As their child began to get a little older, there was a strain between Ken and Frances. They often differed on how to handle the child's misbehavior. Frances preferred to remove temptations from her little boy's reach, and Ken felt that his son should learn not to touch things that didn't belong to him. Ken insisted that a slap on the hand was the only way to teach this. Frances hated hitting her child, even just a tap. Their son, Paul, was curious and lively, and she loved that about him.

Being a minister and a minister's wife is not easy, and life under a microscope seemed to take its toll, especially on Ken. The need for constant assurance and reminders that he was good enough shackled him. He wanted to charm everyone. He was imprisoned by every disagreement with the church board, every small critique from older members of the congregation (who felt it was their job to "guide" the wet-behind-the-ears pastor), and every judgment of himself as pastor, husband, or father. This pressure (which he experienced as persecution) made him compel Frances to be even stricter with their little boy, since his behavior would reflect on them. Their little boy was constantly corrected, and Frances worried about the effects on Paul, but Ken's corrections on his son were just a reflection of his harsh judgments on himself.

Ken had desired so much more from himself. Like his favorite movie character, Don Quixote, he had wanted to right unrightable wrongs, to fight the unbeatable foes, to love purely and chastely. These were the desires that sent him into the ministry, partly because he had been born with a truly gentle, compassionate heart and partly because of his deep, unquenchable desire to feel admired and adored, to feel worthy.

Ken's persecutors never realized that every criticism reminded him of his own mother's disgust and of the failures he hid in shame. There was so much shame. Many times, he wondered what people would really think of him if they knew the truth of what was in his mind and heart. He had discovered the soothing effect of sexually explicit images as a young teen. It was something he kept secret from his mother, and it gave him a sense of control. Pornography and the ability to charm women gave him a sense of power and worth. The desperate wives of abusive husbands who came for counseling and the loose women who idealized him for his position of authority and power were all drawn to him. He found himself in constant temptation and began experiencing bouts of depression as he fought the temptation while being constantly criticized. He still could not escape the message "You are just not good enough" and was drawn to behavior that would temporarily ease his pain but then make him feel horribly guilty.

THE IDEALIST'S FRIEND

Frances had been so excited to share her news with her best girlfriend. They did everything together, and Frances imagined the fun they would have together as she prepared for this new baby. She wore pink in hopes it would somehow foreshadow the birth of her first little girl. Frances's oldest son was a daddy's boy. He loved Mommy, but Daddy was his idol. She longed for that honor with her next child.

At first, Frances's friend seemed excited about her pregnancy and happy for her, but as the months went on, her friend began to cancel their plans, seemingly too busy for her. One night, lying next to her husband in their bed, Frances put her hand on his shoulder. She knew Ken was tired, but she couldn't get it out of her mind. She was losing her best friend, and she didn't understand why.

As Frances continued to press Ken to talk about it, she could see his frustration increasing. She touched her pregnant stomach gently. Maybe she was just going through something with her hormones and feeling paranoid. Her self-doubt was quickly replaced with fear as Ken suddenly began hitting her and venting his rage all over her body. He screamed at her. "I told you I don't want to talk about this, but you just go on and on! I said shut up and go to sleep! But you don't stop! You don't ever stop!"

Ken's eyes were dark and frightening, not the loving eyes of the man she knew. It was as if something had taken over his body. Frances's pleas for him to stop were ignored as he kept beating her legs. She sobbed, wrapping her arms around her stomach to protect her unborn child. Thankfully, her husband did not hit her near their baby.

When he finished, Ken rolled away and turned his back to her, shaking in rage. Frances tried to muffle her cries into her pillow, her sobs only intensifying the guilt and the rage that ravaged Ken. His heart pounded, and his hands trembled as he fought his own tears. Ken feared that his mother was right, that he was evil like his father.

Ken did not speak to Frances the next day at the church swim party but stared at her when the church women questioned her about the bruises she could not hide in her swimsuit. Frances looked at her husband. "We were playing around on the couch, and I fell and hit my legs against the floor and table."

The messages Frances had learned in childhood from her parents' situation built a bridge of lies that began that day to cover for her young husband. If the truth came out, everything they had built would be destroyed. The people they had loved and helped would turn against them and perhaps mistakenly against the wondrous God they had shared with them. Her young husband's temper was not from God but was rather a product of his confused childhood. She did not want to hurt anyone else's faith.

Frances had not known why her husband beat her that night. She was confused. Perhaps it was that confusion that let her take him back and forgive him again. What was she to do? She had a baby on the way. She played back that night repeatedly in her mind. What had she done wrong? Surely, she had done something. She would not find the answer to this mystery for many years.

THE CHILDREN

The couple's new baby boy, Tim, arrived shortly before their move to a new church in Flat Rock, Indiana. This child, the only one to inherit the beautiful blue eyes of their ancestors, was quiet and had a watchful eye on everything around him. Tim was quite the opposite of his older brother, Paul, who was all action and activity. Tim would grow to be a listener and a negotiator. He would be a caring big brother to his two sisters who would follow in the next four years. The couple's first girl, Jamie, was all drama and imagination and loved her time alone in her own world, writing stories and creating imaginary people. In comparison, the baby of the family, their little lamb, Christi, clung to her mother's leg and, like her father, desperately yearned for everyone's affections. The people of the church welcomed the family with love and encouragement, and they were truly happy. These parishioners were much kinder than those at other churches and were full of praise and acts of service. Frances and Ken finally had the perfect family, the idealistic life of which Frances always dreamed. These seemed like the ideal years.

PARADISE LOST

"We've been offered a church in Ohio. We're leaving," Ken announced one day. Frances was devastated. Her husband gave her no explanation of why they were moving, but she had promised God she would go where her husband went, so they went.

The people of this new church were harsh in their guidance and often attacked not only Ken, but Frances as well. Ken grew angrier and angrier each time his wife was hurt, but he directed his anger at the church people and his wife. She had to stop being so soft! Her crying reminded him of who he was as a boy. He would never let them make him cry now. Now Ken solved his problems by fighting back.

Frances watched her loving husband fading before her. He argued with the church people and threw tantrums at home in front of his children. Frances began to see that the incidences of temper in the past were not isolated, and she started feeling afraid.

As her mother before her, Frances tried everything she could to keep her husband happy. She catered to his needs while raising four children, running the church nursery school full-time, and performing the duties of a preacher's wife. She gave constantly. Frances tried to help her young husband see that losing his cool with the church people only made things worse. Ken took this as nagging and criticism and soon pulled away from her. The abuse began again, and she struggled to love him more in hopes it would assuage his anger, but it seemed to only make him feel guilty.

It was not long before Ken turned again to the arms of another woman to make him feel powerful and good about himself. The problem was that these feelings were only an illusion. As Ken's life went out of control, he tried to end the relationship. This woman had fallen in love with him, an inconvenience he had not counted on. As he tried to end the affair, she became more distressed. Her small frame shrank away as she developed ulcers and could no longer eat. She had gone to a local doctor for help and confided the truth, not realizing that he was friends with some of the members of the church board.

The church board fired Ken immediately upon learning the truth. He knew he had no choice but to tell Frances. When he confessed the reason for his firing, his young wife fell to the ground. She looked at him with tears pouring down.

THE IDEALIST ALONE

Frances sobbed alone in the darkness of her new home. She could not lift her head from the couch cushion, and the tears streamed down her cheeks. It had been a few months since she had left Ken. How had her life come to this? How had she been so wrong about the man she thought would fulfill her destiny? She believed that he was the man she had prayed for, a man who seemed to be everything she had dreamed of. She thought perhaps she could have forgiven the affair. He had convinced her somehow that she had failed him; however, she could no longer stand his anger and abuse. She left and told him that unless he got help, she would file for divorce. Her heart broke as she thought about the months that she had to stay in that house, watching out the window as the woman who slept with her husband was allowed at church but she and her children were not. She wondered why no one had come to try to help her and her husband work matters out, why they had not helped him recover from his sin. Ken was destroyed by his own actions and cried every time he spoke to Frances on the phone.

Frances's children missed their father. For their sakes, she did not file for the divorce. She held out hope that Ken would get the help he needed and come back. She feared he would come back and not be changed.

Ken called her. He was coming to visit, and she agreed to talk. The phone rang again, and she thought it was him. She picked it up, and at first, it was silent. Then she heard her new best friend's voice trembling. She wanted to warn her—Ken was on his way to Frances's house, and he was furious. Ken had been with Frances's friend, and her friend confessed something sexual had almost happened between them, and she hinted that it was not the first time.

"Why did you stop it?" Frances managed to get out.

Her friend began to cry. "Because I love you more than I love him."

Stunned, Frances hung up the phone. Memories flooded back— memories of the women in their churches and of friends who had suddenly avoided her, the painful memory of the beating she had taken from Ken when he went into a rage over the questions she was asking him about her girlfriend. "Oh dear God," she prayed as she realized that it had not been one affair but many.

THE IDEALIST AND THE FIGHTER

Ken was devastated when the divorce papers arrived. It was enough to send him for help. He received shock treatments for an unnamed psychological disorder, and when he returned to Ohio a year later to visit his children, he seemed better.

Frances did not want him back. She had formed a life of her own. She was dating a kind man, a man who would never hit a woman or lie or cheat but who also did not want to marry a woman with four children. Still, life without Ken was peaceful.

Frances's oldest son had been her right-hand man, helping her with the younger kids, learning to cook, and helping entertain the thirteen children she had taken in for daycare in order to pay the bills. They had become so close, but she sensed a change in him from his father's first visits. Paul had become convinced that if both his mother's friend, who had supposedly lied about his father, and his mother's boyfriend could be chased away, his parents would get back together. He was just a boy, but he had a will the size of the Grand Canyon. He climbed out windows, tied up babysitters, and fought Frances on everything. She knew she could not win. She was losing her child, and nothing was worse to her.

Ken stepped in and appeared to bring calm back to his son's life. His children, who had not understood the reasons for the separation, seemed happier with their parents together, and Frances wanted to believe that the help Ken received had changed him. He seemed calmer, kinder, and more at peace;

he was funny and charming again. She missed their work too. She longed to be back serving God. Slowly, her heart gave way again to forgiveness. She owed it to all of them to try one more time, but this would be the last chance.

Frances and Ken were remarried in her mother's home with their children around them. There was so much joy, so much celebration. Surely this time, their life would be beautiful, loving, and honoring to God.

THE SECOND MARRIAGE OF IDEALIST AND CHARMER

They were no strangers to moving, but their new neighborhood in Pennsylvania was different from anywhere they had ever lived. The house was bigger and offered a downstairs family room where the younger children could run and play. Paul, who was almost twelve, had his own room downstairs, which became his sanctuary. Tim, who was nine, shared his father's movie room, loaded with tons of comic books, plenty to keep a young hero wannabe entertained. At the same time, he was warier of their situation and kept a close eye on his mother. He did not totally trust his father. Jamie, just seven, had an entire playroom for her Barbie dolls with castles and dress-up clothes, a place where she could get lost in her imagination for days. She tried not to think about her father being back. She longed to create her own world away from it all. No one realized how lonely she was in this new place. She would flit through for a quick hug and go back to the world where she felt she belonged, a world none of them knew existed. In that world, she was happy.

It was their little sister who seemed the most lost. The youngest, five-year-old Christi, rarely left her mother's side, like a little lamb, desperate for cuddling and attention. She was more emotional but so loving, and as long as her mother was near, she was happy. Her soul was even softer than those of her tender siblings.

At first, Frances was very happy to see her children back with their father, full of hope and excitement in a new place. It helped her to lower her guard, to let him back in. She had loved Ken so much, and soon, she found herself loving him once more.

THE BULLIES

School was in midseason, and it was hard enough being the new kids, but in this blue-collar area of Pennsylvania, that meant being fresh meat for the school and neighborhood bullies. School was held in a cold, stone building, the playground simply a square slab of cement surrounding the building and fenced off from the street. When the kids walked onto the playground, the other children just stared at them. The oldest three had walked to school those first few days, with Paul in the lead, his younger brother staying back a bit to let their younger sister catch up. They had never imagined that within a few short months, they would fashion weapons out of reeds to protect themselves as they walked to school or did their paper routes. They learned to stay close to one another for protection.

Ken had a challenging ministry in this new place. He could not seem to escape the fear of his past being discovered by his new parishioners. He felt intense stress when he came home every day and heard that his children were being verbally and physically attacked at school. Ken would defend his children with his life. Despite his flaws, he did love them deeply; no one would hurt his children.

THE FLOOD

It broke Frances's heart to see her children struggle. She realized how bad it was when her oldest son, her little fighter, broke down and cried, afraid to go to school on his birthday, and then again when her little girl came home with bloody scratches on her hands from fighting off a female bully on the playground. The stress of living this way was affecting all of them. Frances wanted to leave, but Ken had other ideas. He sat his children down. "I know that your mother and I have taught you children never to hit, and I never want to hear of you starting a fight, but if you have to protect yourself, you do it." Frances shuddered at the thought of her children hitting people. There had been too much hitting in their house already.

The stress was taking a toll on their marriage too. Ken became moody and depressed again, the charm all but gone. The joy they had before the move had left quickly. Then their life was dramatically impacted by a storm—the flood of 1972. The newscasters warned only of slight water damage and encouraged residents to put their valuables on their kitchen tables or higher up in their houses before they evacuated. Ken left his family with a couple from his church whose house was on higher ground. He bravely went with the rest of the men to try to dam up the river, even though he could not swim (he truly did love his family and his life). Their work was futile, and the flood waters were too powerful. With their lives in danger, they had to evacuate as the dike broke. His family was not safe. The waters were worse than anyone had expected, and he hurried to them to help them get to the mall on the mountaintop.

At the mall, they all hugged, realizing how close they had come to losing one another. They prayed that God would help them know what to do. Christi sobbed, and her cries were especially heartbreaking. A manager of one of the mall stores heard the tiny one's voice. He asked if the family had been in the flood. The little girl nodded. He made a call to his wife, and they took them all in and gave them a home. It was not easy with eleven people sharing a home and a small camper, and as they came into the third month, Frances prayed they would finally get a mobile home to stay in until their house was repaired.

"Father," Frances prayed, "please send us a trailer, and please make it a blue one so that my children will know it came from you." That night, they got a phone call. Their trailer was on its way.

As they drove up the driveway where their flooded home stood, Frances smiled. Her children piled out of the car and stared. In their backyard stood a three-bedroom mobile home, a beautiful shade of pale blue.

The lot behind their house also had mobile homes where other families were living. There was an elderly couple, a middle-aged couple, and a young couple with a new baby and a troubled marriage. Ken and Frances set about the business of pastoring their flock with fervor. Ken baptized numerous souls into the kingdom of Jesus Christ, his wife's music ministering comfort to those who had lost their homes, and their congregation grew. The young couple who were living behind them, Frank and Penny, joined the church, and they turned to Ken for counseling. Frances befriended Penny, who was needy and seemed so desperate to have a friend. Jamie cared for Penny's child. They seemed to be reestablishing a community of support and love.

THE IDEALIST FACES REALITY

Frances's hands trembled as she dropped the phone and fell to the floor. She could not control the shaking of her body, and she began to scream and pull on her hair. Her little girls ran into the room and saw their mother writhing on the floor hysterically. Christi, nine years old, sat at her side, pleading for her to be all right, as Jamie, barely eleven, ran to call an ambulance. "It will be OK, Mommy," she said as she stroked her mother's head with one hand and held her little sister with the other. The ambulance arrived, and Jamie ran down the street to get her father from the church. She burst into an elder's meeting, totally unaware that her father was in the process of being fired.

"Mom was talking to Penny on the phone, and she fell down screaming and crying," she announced.

Her father jumped up and grabbed his daughter by the arm, pulling her from the room. His eyes were dark and wild as he violently carted her off. When they arrived home, Jamie ran and hid in the hall closet, a place she often went when her father was mad.

LEAVING PENNSYLVANIA

Frances did not speak as she packed their final belongings. Ken had found a new church in Ohio, and their furniture was already on the way when she had learned the full extent of her husband's relationship with her friend. Her body and heart could not handle anything but getting her children packed and into the car. She had lost so much weight, she could barely help pack the boxes. Her heart sank, and she tried not to think about Penny's words: "If you don't start treating your husband better, he will find someone who will. You need to respect him, treat him like a man." She had tried so hard to honor him, but how do you honor someone who betrays you repeatedly? Frances packed her last box and prayed that somehow she would find the strength to survive this final betrayal. She wanted to die, but how could she leave these beautiful children? She put one foot in front of the other, because it was all she could do.

The new church was in a small town with only two hundred people. In public, in front of the church, Ken and Frances were the perfect couple. They lied. Their children lied. No one would ever have known that behind the scenes, their family was on the brink of disaster.

The violence grew, and soon, their children began to show signs of the distress, most apparent in their youngest son, Tim, who developed ulcers and became quite ill. The effects were less evident in Jamie, who made herself vomit on the days her father stayed home to work because she wanted to stay home from school. She wanted to be there if her father hurt her mother—then he would have to hurt her too. Ken and Frances had no clue of the dark secrets that would creep into the life of their baby, Christi, as well. Christi spent many hours with a best friend who was sweet and kind. Frances was grateful her daughter had a happy place to go. Neither she nor Ken had any idea that in her early teen years, the father of that girl would subject their little girl to inappropriate touching. Christi would say nothing.

SETTING THE IDEALIST FREE

After a night of his parents fighting, thirteen-year-old Tim buckled over in pain, and Frances held him in her arms. He was her boy; theirs had always been a rare connection, and she could not bear that he was suffering. He held his stomach and cried out. The pain of the ulcer was unbearable. She rocked him and prayed for God's help.

When his mother was finally allowed to see him in the emergency room, her little hero looked up at her with his big blue eyes. She stroked his blond curls. He was so young, yet he was carrying so much. It was enough to have to live with his own fears and emotions, but trying to protect his little sisters, trying to be there to support his mother, was too much. They both cried.

"I love my dad," he told her, "but if you stay, I am afraid I will hate him."

She had stayed because she thought it was what was best for her kids and for the church. She had not finished her education, and she didn't know how she would provide for four children on her own, but looking at her little man in a hospital bed, confessing his fears, she began to wonder. Could anything be worse than this?

GETTING AWAY

Frances longed to see her mother, to get herself and her children away for a while. Her mother's tender arms enveloped her, and she could not help but cry. Her mother held Frances tightly, with the strength of a woman who had survived the life her daughter was now facing. Once the children had gone to sleep, her mother took her daughter's slender hand. She could feel her bones. She could see the weight she had lost from her face and the darkness around her eyes.

"You know that I wanted you to do everything you could to make your marriage work," her mother said, "but I am afraid you will not survive this. If you don't leave him, I am afraid you will die."

In her mother's eyes, she saw the memories of her brother. She relived her mother's pain at losing a child. Frances knew that for all her hope that things would get better, hope was not enough to cause her mother the pain of losing another child. It was not enough to risk Tim hating his father. Frances did not hate Ken. She felt sorry for him. Ken had taken every good gift God had given him and destroyed it, because in his tortured soul, he could never feel loved. Frances had loved him the best she knew how, but her love would never be enough. It was time to let him go. Ken would now experience her rejection for the final time.

Ken, rejected and alone, full of anger, guilt, and shame, wondered about his future. He had turned to the wrong things for comfort. He had tried to use his charm to build protection from the criticism, to soothe his soul from the persecution, only to discover that his actions created more pain. One can only imagine the level of self-persecution he felt, alone with his thoughts, alone with his failure, alone.

CHAPTER 6

....

ARE YOU A CHARMER?

UNDERSTANDING THE CHARMER

THE CHARMING SOFT SOUL IS FULL OF CHARISMA. CHARMERS HAVE TWINKLES IN their eyes and draw people to them like magnets. They are often funny and attractive and fascinate others with their personality and stories. Others find themselves captivated by the Charmers' wit and allure. Charmers are energetic and motivating. When you are around a Charmer, you are entertained and often motivated to do what he or she says to do. Charmers can be incredible public speakers with the uncanny ability to motivate and inspire a crowd. This type of soft soul can persuade others to perform remarkable acts of courage and help them strive toward great goals.

Just as Charmers can lead people to perform wonderful actions, they also can manipulate others for their own purposes. If the world has been cruel to a Charmer, they can become overly self-focused and capable of deceit and persuading others for their own benefit. The same natural abilities that can inspire others can also cause quite a bit of harm to others when the Charmer leads them to actions that are unhealthy or wrong. Charmers who have been scarred by the world are capable of treating people like objects and at times will take on the attitude that the "ends justify the means." When that happens, Charmers often become manipulators. In literature and other archetypal studies, the Charmer shows characteristics similar to the magician, the shaman, and the healer.

Major Tendencies

Charmers seek attention. They want to make others notice them in order to prove that they are worthwhile. They are very sensitive to others' opinions and react with either devastation or anger when persecuted or ignored. Charmers tend to be attracted to roles and careers that are connected with being in the spotlight, entertaining others, or generating praise.

The Positive Aspects

What is admirable about Charmers is that they want to entertain others and make an impact. They want to see others smile. What a beautiful thing! They fight to make themselves better people despite their failures. Their soft souls often truly want to do good and make the world a better place.

The Shadow Side

In their never-ending quest for attention, Charmers can make choices that lead to hurt relationships. Their insatiable need for attention becomes poisonous when that attention is negative or others see them as bad or unworthy. It can be devastating for them when they are persecuted or rejected. The shame can turn into anger in an attempt to avoid facing their own "failure" at being a good person. At times, Charmers who are victimized can later become victimizers.

Charmers try to soothe the pain of their persecution with attention from others in whatever form can make them feel loved and be seen as good. They often focus on seeking approval from people of the same gender as their rejecting or overly critical parent. At times, this can lead to love or sex addictions.

Strategies for Integrating Your Soft Soul While Honoring Your Charming Tendencies

- See your own goodness—you can't expect others to see the good in you if you don't see it first. If you need to, keep a journal of the things you have done well, and when you feel insecure, go to that journal for a reminder that you can do good, moral, and positive things.

- Choose relationships based not on how they make you feel, but rather on how healthy the relationship is. A healthy relationship will not bring humiliation to you or to others. When temptation calls, it is not cowardly but shows true wisdom to turn and run.

- Walk away from any behavior that does not fit with your spiritual beliefs. Use your ability to charm and persuade to lead others to things that are *good* for them!

- Admit your humanness and know that just because you are capable of bad deeds does not mean you are bad—everyone fails. That is the beauty of God's grace. We all do a mixture of good and bad in our lives, and the key is to continually strive to do more acts that honor God and help others than acts that cause harm.

- Remember that shame is selfish and does not serve the world. Shame is just about you. Instead of feeling shame, choose to feel conviction and make amends to anyone you have harmed, either intentionally or unintentionally.

- Repair your wounds. If you experience rejection and live with messages from childhood about not being good enough, seek out help from a life coach, therapist, or friend to heal. But don't stay focused on the past; rather, focus on creating a spectacular future.

CHAPTER 7

SOFT SOULS WHO WANT THINGS TO BE FAIR AND JUST

The Story of a Fighter

THE FIGHTER

Paul was not surprised by his parents' second divorce. In fact, he was relieved. He saw it coming, and he was tired of what he felt were the lies that the family had to live. Lies are wrong, and he knew this. He wondered how his father and mother could justify the false image that he believed they presented to the public. Paul thought of all of the times he was asked to hold back from sharing with the church congregation what was going on in his family. He could not speak of the previous divorce. He could not speak of the affair at the last church. And now, despite the fact that his mother had been out of the house for some time, he was asked not to speak of the second divorce. Fearful of losing his job, Ken would announce it only when he needed to share it with the church. Being separated was not as bad as getting divorced, so as far as the parishioners knew, Ken and Frances would soon reconcile. Nevertheless, when Paul was confronted by one of his friends who had read about the divorce in the Columbus newspaper (it was not announced in their small town newspaper), he thought, *This will be the last time I lie for them.*

Little did Paul know that the anger that he had about the hypocrisy of their lives would lead to a life of pursuing justice. He would live a life where things would be made right. If someone hurt him, he would hurt them back. If someone threatened him, he would threaten them back until they stopped. He would win all fights. It would be his motto for most of his life. Paul was determined he would never lose; he would be a fighter.

THE FIGHTER'S BEGINNINGS

"Meningitis." The word hung in the air over the young couple. It was a deadly disease, one that took the lives of grown men, yet they watched their little boy in his hospital bed, hanging on against the pain, against the fevers. He was a fighter. He would not go easily. As his fever rose to a dangerous level, his little body quivered, and he could barely cry. The doctors were not hopeful.

As they held their small son, his thick, dark hair lay against his skin, red from fever. He was so beautiful to them, so perfect. How could the doctors say they might be leaving the hospital without him? They were both so young to be dealing with this, too young. Ken was only twenty-one and Frances nineteen. How could God ask them to handle giving up their infant son before they had a chance to know him?

Paul's mother wept with tears that came from the deepest, most vulnerable place in her soul, and his father wept too as he wrapped her in his arms. Their son might be dying, and it was unbearable. They prayed together, while in another room, their tiny fighter continued his battle to live.

It is easy to say that you have faith when problems are small and insignificant, but to have enough faith to put your only son into God's hands and pray that His will be done is one of the hardest things any parent can do. The doctor's predictions for the outcome were bleak. He spoke of brain damage and the possibility of their son being unable to function on his own. Frances still wanted her child. She didn't care. She thought she could bear anything more than his death. The little fighter's illness was the first of many tests her faith would bear in the years to come. She loved God; He had been her shelter and her refuge. Given that truth, how could she not trust Him with her most precious son? Frances went to Ken, and together, they knelt and offered Paul to God for His will to be done. They cried in each other's arms, for at the time, they were each other's best friend and greatest love. That day on their knees together, they had offered up God's greatest gift, though it had been the hardest day of their young lives. Within a few hours, their son's fever broke—God had given him back to them.

A LITTLE COWBOY

You would have never known that Paul started out a sick baby. He had developed seizures at the age of five, but the only thing that testing showed was that his brain waves were a little faster than normal. After about a year, the seizures stopped, and he never dealt with them again.

After recovering from meningitis, he could best be described as active. His parents called him "Deputy Doodle" as he ran around the yard in his cowboy hat and boots. The fighter looked like his father, who was his idol, but had a beautiful smile like his mother. He was a sweet boy who wanted to kiss everyone. He was loving, expressive, and excitable. He liked to touch things, to figure out how things worked. This often contrasted with his father's view of how he should behave, and he was punished. But he was a daddy's boy, and in his eyes, his father could do no wrong.

WINTER

At only two years old, Paul struggled to climb up to the windowsill. He was incredibly excited and called several times for his daddy to look at the snow. He pointed his tiny finger outside. "No, Daddy, no."

His father had been deep in an emotional struggle that day and, mistakenly thinking that his two-year-old was telling him no, he yanked his young son up and spanked him. "You don't tell me no."

Paul's brown eyes, so like his own, looked heartbroken. In tears, the tiny boy tried to make his intentions clear. He pointed to the window, and his mother realized that he had been trying his best to say, "Snow, Daddy, snow." Ken's face grew red with shame for what he had done to the boy, and Frances hoped it would stop her husband from being so quick to spank him.

"My son will be good," Ken insisted defensively. His son would try his very best to be just that. He wanted his father's approval more than anything, but he was a little boy, full of energy and gumption, and soon, he would fail.

RESOLUTIONS

Every New Year's Eve, the question was the same. "What are you going to do to be a better boy next year?" Ken would ask Paul. The little boy hated that question. *When will I be good enough just for who I am?* he would silently ask himself. *Have I really been that bad this year?* he continued to ponder. Later in his life, Paul would no longer accept or ask himself that question. He would refuse to admit the need to do anything better. He would give it everything he could and felt like he always did the right thing, but as a young boy, Paul took the question very seriously. Whether he felt he was wrong or not, he always came up with something that he was failing at, if for no other reason than to give his father the satisfaction of feeling as if he was improving his son.

FIGHTING THE DIVORCE

When Ken and Frances first got divorced, it was hardest on Paul. He loved his father so deeply, and to protect Ken, Frances did not tell the children the true reason for their divorce. In Paul's eyes, he felt his mother was being unjust. He remembered her following his father, trying often to correct his behavior or his thinking. He felt she was a nag. He had no idea what his mother had gone through or why she tried so hard to keep her husband's temper under control. He only knew she had wanted the separation. It was her fault that he was separated from his father, Paul thought. But his parents had taught him respect, and at first, Paul would support his mother, as now he was the man of the house.

It was when his father returned from being away that Paul became confused. His once-powerful father was now deeply depressed and would cry in front of him, saying how much he missed his family. His pain was palpable and intense, and Paul could not bear to see him that way. Paul's anger toward his mother grew. He became angry and rebellious, and eventually, he became too much for Frances to handle. He fought her every step of the way and was thrilled when his parents remarried.

MOVING TO PENNSYLVANIA

Once Ken and Frances remarried, life seemed to return to normal. The family moved to Pennsylvania, and Paul was given his own room in the basement where he could have solitude. He was drawn to hunting and taxidermy. As a young teen, he made his own shells for his guns and loved going out shooting. He was a young man who would have fit in during the Wild West, as he loved all things rustic and of the earth. He despised how neat they had to keep their house and proclaimed that one day, he would live in a more rugged environment.

Paul was removed from his siblings both logistically and emotionally. Jamie and Christi were too young for him to hang out with, and his brother, Tim, was as different from him as any brother could be. Tim was all innocent in the eyes of Frances and could always get Paul into trouble. When they would fight, Paul could always beat Tim with pure physical strength, but Tim could win at times by being sneakier than his brother. They would be fighting or wrestling, and when it looked like Paul would win, Tim would run at him and jump up into the air, kicking him in the chest with his feet. This would knock Paul to the floor as Tim ran to Frances, complaining about how Paul was picking on him. Because Tim was so slight compared to Paul, Frances would always take his side and lecture Paul on how he needed to be nicer to his brother. Paul hated the injustice of this.

The new school was challenging, and Paul (who did not really love fighting at this point in his life) was being bullied daily by a larger boy. He told his father about it, and Ken, tired of his children being hurt, encouraged Paul to fight back. Paul's fists were pounding the boy's face when the principal ran out of the school to stop the fight. Paul had made his point. The boy never bothered him again. This was a pivotal moment for Paul. He had stood up for himself. He would never again go back to being that soft boy who let others hurt and humiliate him. He would never lose a fight. He would do whatever it took to win.

HIS FATHER'S SON

Ken stood at the pulpit, and Paul looked around the church at all the people watching his dad. His father had power over the crowd. All eyes were on Ken. Paul longed to communicate in a way that captivated people. He had much to say and so much he wanted to share. Though Paul would battle when needed, he would only do so when he perceived injustice. At his core, he wanted to help people. Soon, he would learn to play the guitar and start singing in church. He felt the songs deeply and had no problem showing tears in front of the parishioners from the security and safety of the stage. Paul's performance came from his heart and was a perfect combination of his father's ability to move an audience and his mother's musical giftedness. Paul loved singing. He would sing with his grandmother and record music with her playing the piano. He and his mother also connected around song. While his parents were married, Paul would often perform in their church with his siblings singing with him (and sometimes playing the tambourine horribly). He wanted to move the audience with his voice and heart. At one point in his life, he decided to dedicate his life to singing. That desire, however, just became another struggle for Paul.

THE FIGHTER'S LOVE FOR THE CHARMER

The marriage of Frances and Ken continued to struggle in those years, and at times, Paul would be on the receiving end of his father's anger. He did not doubt that his father loved him. Paul adored his father. After the second divorce, he stayed with him and cherished those years of being connected to Ken. He experienced his father's patience when he taught him how to drive. He knew how much it meant to his father when he kissed him good-bye on the cheek in view of the church people. Paul shared wonderful trips and talks with his father. He specifically loved a handwritten letter his father wrote him after the second divorce. "Thank you for staying with me even though I did wrong. I have to write this to you, because I would cry if I had to say it to you. I love you." He had his father's approval; all was right and just.

Paul had difficulty in school. His intelligence was more practical than book related. He could take anything apart and put it back together. He was a builder. Paul did not enjoy books or the constraints of traditional education. Some teachers labeled him as difficult, yet another challenge he had to face and overcome. Around seventh grade, Paul decided to follow a vocational path and ended up specializing in welding. However, he was strongly attracted to Christian music. Eventually, he graduated and went to college to train for his musical career. Not surprisingly, he chose the same Bible college that his parents attended but again struggled with the academic expectations and what he thought were ridiculous and wasteful teachings. Paul quit college and decided to pursue singing in churches across the country. He booked a few events, asking only for donations as payment, but again, like most everything else in his life, this became a battle. Paul had sent out three hundred letters to churches in Ohio and only received one response. He had expected churches to welcome him warmly and was very disappointed in their response. Paul became angry and looked to pursue another career.

He decided to work for a security company guarding buildings, offices, banks, and factories and found that he enjoyed the work. This led him to look into law enforcement, a field that naturally spoke to his strong sense of justice.

THE FIGHTER AND THE HIGHWAY PATROL

Paul started highway patrol training with a class of ninety-one cadets. Only thirty-nine completed the difficult experience. The training was similar to the military, where they try to break you down to your lowest point before they build you into the person they want you to be. During his training, Paul experienced sleep deprivation, mind games, and ridiculous tasks. He endured it, fighting through any temptation to quit. Every weekend as Paul typed his summary of the activities for the week, he would break into tears, but then he would go back and face anything they had to throw at him.

Paul stood across from his opponent in the State Highway Patrol Academy, and his mind was a mix of emotions. They were teaching the cadets to box, and the person's gender was irrelevant. As he looked at the young woman across from him, he wondered if he could do it. He had never hit a woman. The officer in charge of the training ordered him to hit her. He took a small jab. "Hit her harder!" the officer commanded. Paul hesitated. "Hit her harder!" He pulled back his arm and punched her in the face. She went down on the ground. The members of the patrol cheered his victory.

That night, despite being in his twenties, he returned to the home he shared with his mother and siblings and cried in his mother's arms.

The years in the highway patrol were good years for Paul. Here was a chance to enforce justice. Here was a chance to make things right and fight all wrongs. They did their best to break him, but he was tough and unbreakable. On his first day as a rookie cop, he was called to the scene of a horrible accident and handed a bag. "What's in here?" Paul asked the seasoned patrolman.

"Oh, that's the head of the victim from the accident. It was sliced right off. We want you to walk around with it for a while," the officer responded.

They expected Paul to freak out and be upset. The cop in him took over; he calmly walked the bag with the presumed head over to the patrol car and put it in the back seat.

The highway patrol went to great lengths to teach him how to shut off his emotions. To them, emotions represented weakness and could put your life in danger at any moment. You had to be logical and suspicious to survive. When you pulled someone over for speeding, you expected the person to lie to you. When you entered a domestic violence situation, you trusted no one. If you were met with aggression, you retaliated with greater force than the other person did. These were lessons that would save a patrolman's life in the line of duty. They were not lessons that would always help in relationships outside of work.

Two years later, Paul was designated the primary investigator of a fatality for the first time. A woman had been killed in a car accident, and the driver would not admit that he had been behind the wheel. Paul felt a huge responsibility for doing the investigation correctly. As he took measurements and interviewed people, he found himself growing angrier. He was furious at the irresponsibility of the driver and could not fathom how someone could be so careless as to get a loved one killed. He made a vow to himself to do whatever he could to prevent these terrible accidents.

Today, when Paul speaks of his time in the highway patrol, he talks about how it matured him so he was no longer the "wimpy preacher's kid." He goes on to say, "They made me what they wanted me to be, decisive and not taking any crap! Since then, all of my decisions have worked out right because I do what is right." Paul sees nothing wrong with being a fighter. In fact, he relishes the role. "I'm not going to roll over like all of those other people out there. No one is going to take advantage of me!" he has often been heard to say. Paul got over being that boy who cried in his mother's arms after hitting the woman. He became tough and proud and would never be hurt by anyone again. At least, that is what he thought.

THE FIGHTER'S FIRST WIFE

One thing that Paul discovered being on the highway patrol was that women love a man in uniform. He dated frequently but never had deep feelings for anyone. One day, while eating at a McDonald's in uniform, he was approached by a cute, blond-haired woman who started flirting with him. After six months of dating, they got married. Soon though, the differences in their ages and perspectives started showing up in their relationship. Paul wanted a traditional wife, and she wanted freedom and independence. Paul stopped working overtime and wanted to put his marriage first. He wanted to be with her all the time.

They traveled constantly, taking many vacations and visiting fantastic places. However, their marriage was full of fighting and pain. When Paul's shift was changed, he wanted his wife to quit working so they would have time together. He wanted her to be home with him and to commit her entire self to their marriage, just as he felt he was willing to do. That level of commitment was right; anything less than that was wrong in his eyes. "This was the way marriage was meant to be," Paul would often claim. He found her distant and stubborn. In turn, she found him controlling and intrusive, feeling as if she could never have a moment to herself. This resulted in her pushing him away.

Paul became frustrated and angry. His anger only pushed her further away as she would use that as justification to do whatever she wanted. They met several times with Ken and Tim, who tried to counsel them on what each of them could do differently, but nothing seemed to help. With her frequent disappearances, Paul began to suspect that his wife was seeing another trooper. He tried everything he could think of to get her to change. Toward the end, he even tried ignoring her, hoping that this would bring her affection back to him, but it did not work. One Tuesday, he finally had enough of screaming and cussing at his wife. He told her that if she did not like living with him, she should just leave.

Shortly after that conversation, she packed her belongings, took the dog, and left him. Paul came home to find a note on his kitchen table; their relationship was over.

FIGHTING THE SYSTEM

During his marriage difficulties, Paul was clashing with others on multiple battlefields. While on vacation with his wife, the Humane Society came and took all of the animals from his property (cats, dogs, and a goat), claiming that he was neglecting them. Paul had asked a friend to come over to take care of the animals, but the friend had only stopped by a few times, and a neighbor reported the situation. When Paul returned home, he could not get the Humane Society to return his animals, and it turned into a huge and expensive legal battle. The Humane Society even went as far as to call Paul's commanding officer at home to complain about Paul's behavior, and the officer then became involved in the court situation. Whether it was the frustration over becoming involved in the trial or complaints received accusing the highway patrol of fixing the trial, Paul felt like his superiors started treating him differently at this point. Despite his seniority, they took away his new patrol car and gave him an older one, claiming that he was not taking good care of the newer car. They changed his shift to one he did not like. He was verbally reprimanded for doing something that his supervisor approved. It appeared as though they were looking to do anything to irritate him.

The final blow came when, during four days that Paul had off, he went to another county sheriff's office to see if he could help with an investigation. A town marshal and friend of his had been murdered, and Paul wanted to help bring the criminal to justice. News of his involvement got back to his superiors, and Paul was accused of interfering with a murder investigation. He was then given a formal reprimand for leaving an orange juice bottle in his patrol car and was told that he was going to face disciplinary action for going to the other sheriff's office. That night, Paul quit his career of seven and a half years. He refused to play by their rules. They were not just, they were not fair, and he would no longer subject himself to their authority.

During this tough time and before the dissolution of his marriage was final, Paul contacted his former Bible college and said that he wanted to return to school. When he received the application, he saw that the section on marital status stated, "If divorced, give reasons why on a separate piece of paper." Paul simply wrote, "Will be final on September 29." In response, he received two letters from the college informing him that they could not process his application without further information regarding his divorce. This infuriated Paul. "Who are they to decide if I can come back to school or not given what I say about the divorce?" Paul confronted them on the phone about the question. They responded that he may not be admitted to the college if he had committed adultery, which enraged him even more. Another person may have just clarified that he had not been unfaithful, but Paul saw the question as intrusive and wrong. "How dare you judge!" he claimed, and he refused to fill out the information. This would be a theme for Paul; he would never back down from what he thought was right. He would never compromise his beliefs. No one would control him, no one would hurt him, and he would win at all costs.

THE FIGHTER'S ISOLATION YEARS

After singing at churches for a while, he moved to a farm that had been in the family for decades. For this period of his life, Paul would live alone, a man in the wilderness. No one knows much about the six years he spent in solitude, healing as he lived off the land. While living on the farm, he hunted when he was hungry, built a fire when he needed to cook food, and had limited contact with anyone who was not family.

This environment seemed the most healing for Paul. Like a man born in an earlier time, he was a survivalist and did not need the comforts that others seemed to cherish. It was man versus the wilderness, just the way

Paul liked it. Roughing it was not a problem for Paul; it was a way of life. He relished it the way pioneers of the past had. In many ways, he belonged in another time, when men hunted for their food, chopped wood, and protected their families from harm, a time when family was everything and men and women only had each other and no one else to rely on in the wilderness. It was the relationship he had sought in his own life but failed to find in his marriage. He was a man's man, different from the sensitive little toddler he had been so many years ago. Yet his heart was still tender, and he did learn to cry again in these years.

To him, living in the woods was heaven, but after six years of solitude, he decided to return to the outside world to find another career.

THE SECOND MARRIAGE

When Paul returned to civilization, he attended chiropractic college. He was gifted with his hands but again struggled with the academic requirements. Paul had tried to find a woman who was willing to love him in the way he wanted to be loved and initially thought he had found her. However, he soon felt his second wife was worse than his first, hiding things from him and even more adamant about her independence. *Doesn't anyone understand what marriage is supposed to be?* he pondered. They fought often, and their love quickly faded. Whether it was the difficulties of the school environment or the strain of his marriage and subsequent divorce, his chiropractic career ended before he was able to graduate. To him, this was the final straw when it came to relationships. In his eyes, every woman he had ever been with had failed to live up to the image of what he wanted in a wife. Again, Paul decided to return to the land and heal.

THE LESSONS HE LEARNED

The highway patrol had taught him a lesson. "If someone hurts me, they are going to wish they had not started a fight," he would proudly claim. "You survive better by being the winner rather than rolling over. I will make it right. I will not let people get away with doing me wrong. They will pay." These words often would come out of Paul's mouth, so much so that his siblings wondered what had happened to that sweet little boy, that "Deputy Doodle," that loving child. Had Paul been hurt so much that his heart just had to hide? After being on the highway patrol, Paul rarely showed tears. When he was hurt, his rage would explode as he claimed his enemies were "stupid," the women who had wronged him were "whores," and the people who did not see the right way to do something were "idiots." His family knew that his heart was still there, but it had been crushed by so many that a wall built of righteousness and anger was erected to protect him from feeling the pain. He would never go out of his way to hurt someone; in fact, he always wanted to help others. Yet if you hurt him, he would get revenge and balance the scales.

There was one place, however, that he allowed himself to be tender, and that was on stage. On the occasions when he was able to sing in a church, he would shed tears, sobbing in front of the audience as he talked about the losses and hurts in his life. Perhaps the protection that came from being removed from the group allowed him to share his heart. Perhaps it was because, there on stage, his pain had a meaning and a purpose. Maybe he was simply willing to show his vulnerability because that little boy who so badly wanted to love and be loved by others was able to express himself in song.

THE CHARMER'S DIAGNOSIS

During these many years of challenge and betrayal, Paul also went through his toughest experience. His cell phone rang, and it was his younger brother, Tim. Paul was expecting a call because their father had gone in for surgery. His skin was turning yellow, and no one could figure out what was wrong with him. Paul was not overly concerned; he figured that it was just something minor and that the call was made to tell him that his father was fine and they had fixed the problem. However, Tim sounded choked up on the phone and was having problems talking. All he could say was "Dad has cancer." Paul's heart sank; surely, his brother was wrong. "What are you talking about?" he asked. Tim responded, telling his brother that they had discovered pancreatic cancer and had removed parts of many organs to contain it. After discussing it a little further, Paul hung up the phone and started making plans to go see his father.

Ken's battle with cancer was intense, and Paul was by his side as often as he could make the trip. He would do anything for his father, and he lost track of the number of times Ken had been admitted for treatment. Family always meant so much to Paul, and he loved his father deeply.

Paul did whatever he could to help his father. Once, he held Ken's tiny body in his arms. He could feel every bone. His dad was a little, shriveled, weak man, crying out in pain. The bedsheets had not been changed for weeks, and his father was in intense pain. Paul offered to pick him up and hold him as the hospital staff changed the sheets. He hooked the urine bag to his pocket and told his father that this needed to be done. "Go ahead. I'm dying anyway," Ken softly mumbled.

Paul was not a fighter now. He was just a boy who loved his father.

He held his father tenderly as the staff changed the bedsheets. It was something that he could do, hold his father in his arms so he would be in less pain as they moved him. He gently laid his father back down, tears in his eyes. "I love you, Dad," he choked out.

His father could barely speak. His voice was feeble, but he whispered, "I love you too."

He did not want to leave, but Paul had to return home. He glanced back at his father as he was leaving the room. A memory flashed in his mind of when he was a young man and he and Ken were visiting a man in the hospital. The man was terminally ill with cancer. After the man's funeral, his father had turned to him and said, "Don't ever let me get that way." Paul wanted to honor his father's wish, but the fighter worried that this was just the way his father would die.

CHAPTER 8

....

ARE YOU A FIGHTER?

UNDERSTANDING THE FIGHTER

A T FIRST, YOU MAY NOT SEE THE FIGHTER AS A TYPE OF SOFT SOUL, BUT remember that we are talking about the ways that people try to protect their soft souls from harm. Also, soft souls are defined not only by gentleness, but also by their deep emotions and caring. Fighters care deeply. They are passionate about justice and doing what is right. They defend the weak, protect the unprotected, and take on causes with persistency and dedication. They are determined and will face seemingly unbeatable opposition for a worthy cause. Fighters never shy away from conflict or battle. They will stand up to anyone who is hurting others, doing what is wrong, or contributing to injustice in the world. Fighters are centered in their passion for righteousness. They have the tenacity to keep at a challenge when others might have given up much sooner. The world needs Fighters who are willing to make it a better place.

When the world has been especially harsh on a Fighter, sometimes he or she sees battles where none exist. That pursuit for righteousness can become overly aggressive, and the Fighter starts fighting for a personal win rather than for the good of the world. Others may feel bullied by Fighters and actually start fearing them (especially other soft souls who are more peaceful in their approach to life). And when wounded Fighters face battles that they can't win, they can move their focus to at least taking down their opponents as they also take the fall. The Fighter is also referred to as the warrior, the soldier, the hero, and the winner.

Major Tendencies

While Idealists can at times repress their pain by focusing on only the positive, Fighters repress by focusing on the battle. Fighters see battles everywhere. They see injustice and want to correct it. They can be assertive at best and overly aggressive at worst. Fighters are driven to right all wrongs and usually feel like they are right.

The Positive Aspects

The world needs Fighters. We need people who are willing to stand up and battle righteously while others cower. The intentions of Fighters are positive, and when they take the correct actions, Fighters can change this world for the better. Fighters show courage in the face of danger and show strength when others flee in fear.

The Shadow Side

What seems like assertiveness to the Fighter can be perceived as aggressiveness by other people. Often, Fighters cause others to feel uncomfortable by the strength of their convictions and the black-and-white nature of their viewpoints and language. The shadow side of their assertiveness and love for justice is that they can appear arrogant or hostile and hurt people unintentionally while focusing on their quest. They can appear unempathetic and can often push away others who do not see right and wrong the same way that they see it. At times, they escalate the battle too quickly. Their fear of being a coward or having others "win" can create intensity in conflict.

Strategies for Integrating Your Soft Soul While Honoring Your Fighting Tendencies

- As a Fighter, the first thing you might consider is that justice does not always occur on this planet. (The authors believe that it will only truly happen in eternity.) There will always be injustice on earth, and we must choose our battles wisely. If we battle everything and everyone, we will end up alone.

- If you find yourself full of anger about how unfair the world can be, learn some tactics for releasing that anger. Discover a strategy (some are shared later in this book) that is healthy and brings you peace.

- When you do need to fight, try to mirror a three-way lightbulb where each click represents a different level of intensity. The first time, be gentle, patient, and kind as you try to correct a person or a situation. If the pattern continues, turn up the heat a little bit and be more assertive. If you have addressed the pattern multiple times and the injustice keeps occurring, only now is it appropriate to bring intensity and strength to the battle.

- Remember while you battle to also choose to love. Build people up rather than just letting them know where they are wrong. Few people change or see your point if they feel attacked by you.

- Also, it is very helpful for the Fighter to find a main cause for which to fight. It should be a cause that is needed, noble, and fulfills your soft soul's desire to make something right.

CHAPTER 9

....

SOFT SOULS
WHO LONG FOR PEACE

The Story of a Pleaser

THE PLEASER

....

His sisters referred to him as their hero, but in truth, he was simply someone who wanted everyone to be happy. He wanted peace for his family. So as Tim sat alone in Ken's hospital room, holding his father's hand as he slept, he looked at the skeleton of a man who had replaced his fifty-two-year-old father, and tears streamed down his face. His father was dreaming and started screaming, "Get away from me! Leave me alone!" Tim stroked his father's head and, in his most soothing voice, said, "Dad, it's OK. I'm here with you, and nothing is after you. Everything is all right. I'm here. I'm here." His father calmed down and went back into a peaceful slumber. The doctors had just increased Ken's morphine because he was in so much pain, and the nightmares were happening more and more frequently. After two years of fighting the cancer, the prognosis for Ken was not good. Tim felt powerless, just as he always did. He knew he could not save his father. He knew he could not bring peace to his father's soul. "Not now, oh God, not now; we were just getting close. God, I can't lose him yet," Tim prayed. Yet some prayers are not answered with a yes.

THE PLEASER'S BEGINNINGS

The dream was intense, frequent, and always the same. He was surrounded by people he loved. Sometimes, it was his family. Sometimes, it was that cute girl he was interested in talking to (but never had the nerve to). The dream would begin with some benign scene of a class or a picnic. Tim was in his disguise as a mild-mannered nerd (which, of course, he was in real life) when suddenly, crooks and murderers would crash into the scene. Tim would quickly duck out of the room to change into his superhero costume before storming back in to take care of the bad guys. However, each time, every single time, his powers would fail him. He was powerless and could not save the ones he loved. It was a constant reminder of his powerlessness in his real life, and he would always awaken frightened, sad, and frustrated. People were unhappy around him, their home had no peace, and he could do nothing about it.

A MILD-MANNERED BOY

As a child, Tim was gentle and loving and just wanted everyone to get along. He loved to sit in the backseat of the family's station wagon, twirling his mother's hair in his fingers. He used to play dolls with Jamie and had fun tickle fights with the baby of the family, Christi. He was somewhat feminine as a child, and his bond with his mother was special and strong. She would always build him up, as she freely expressed words of affirmation and showed affection with her hugs and her time. Her favorite comment about Tim, even when he became an adult, was "You've never caused me an ounce of pain." That made the pleaser so happy. However, when he was young, his relationship with his father was a different matter.

Ken was an athlete, and Tim always suspected that he was too weak in his father's eyes. He remembers his father's temper and how he would run to his sisters' room to comfort them when Ken was on a rampage. Tim always hated arguments and hated to see girls cry. Humor became his defense. He became very good at reading emotions and comforting people. For some reason, he and his father had difficulty connecting. Was it Tim's softness? Was it the fact that Tim was so close to Frances? Or was it simply because of Ken's inner torments? Tim always assumed it was because there was something wrong with him and that he was a disappointment to his father. He was weak, he was gentle, and he just wanted peace; he was not a real man. He felt that he could not please his father.

One evening, he saw his father sitting in the dark. Ken was obviously hurting and depressed. Tim wanted so badly to comfort his father, so he slowly walked up to him, put his arms around his father's neck, and whispered, "Are you OK, Daddy?" He was shocked as his father violently knocked him away and merely said, "Your breath stinks." Tim had no power to comfort his father. With shoulders slumped and spirit crushed, he retreated to his bedroom and pulled out his comic book collection to read stories of heroes who had the power to make a difference and were not weak and ineffectual like him.

The first divorce was difficult for Tim. He, like his siblings, did not understand why his father no longer lived with them, and the stress took a toll on Tim's psyche. He began sleepwalking and struggled with sadness and confusion. During this time, Tim experienced bullying for the first (but not the last) time. Perhaps it was his gentle nature, slight depression, or his small stature, but kids seemed to love to pick on him and reject him. Even for his sisters, he found that he could only be the hero emotionally and not physically. One day, Jamie and Christi ran into their grandmother's house with tears in their eyes as they talked about a bunch of boys picking on them. Tim jumped off the couch and ran with his sisters to confront the bullies. However, when he arrived, there were five of them, and they started throwing rocks at Tim and his sisters. The three of them ran away. Later that night, Tim cried himself to sleep for his weakness and inability to protect those he loved. This sensitivity and tenderness seemed to irritate Ken.

Another time, Tim returned home in tears and told his father about three bullies who were pushing him around. Tim hoped his father would simply hold him and tell him that he loved him for the tender boy that he was. Instead, Ken reacted with anger and disgust. "Can you take one of them in a fight?" he asked Tim.

Multiple thoughts raced through his head, and none of them would justify his response to his father. "Yes, I could take one of them!" he deceitfully declared to the angry pastor.

"Then let's go!" his father said as he grabbed Tim by the arm and took him to their car. For thirty minutes, Tim and his father drove around looking for the boys. Ken hoped they would find them, and Tim secretly and desperately prayed to God that they would be nowhere in sight. They never found them.

When his parents decided to remarry, Tim was happy but hesitant. Despite his concerns, he was willing to go through the loss of moving again from Ohio to Pennsylvania. Throughout the losses, Tim found comfort in the fantasy world of comic books. Tim loved comic books. There were challenges, but the good guy always won, and everyone admired the hero! He and his best friend traded comics, shared favorite stories, created their own superhero movie, and even patrolled the neighborhood on their bikes, armed with firecrackers to help defeat the bad guys (if they ever found one, which they thankfully did not). They had a magical relationship, the kind you find with twelve-year-old boys who think the world is their playground. In those days, it was common for the boys to play on the train tracks, putting pennies on the track for the trains to cross. They even lived out the scene from the Rob Reiner movie *Stand by Me*, where they stupidly and desperately ran across a bridge while a train came barreling at them. They barely made it and never attempted that feat again, simply thankful that their poor judgment did not end in a tragedy. Life was an adventure and one well worth living. At this time, Tim's family seemed happy.

UNIVERSAL MONSTERS

The pinnacle of Tim's young experience came when he and his best friend created a four-minute movie called *London Fog and the Scarecrow vs. Dracula*, in which Tim's father played Dracula. It showed the playful side of Ken. He and Tim bonded around their love for the universal monsters. Tim loved monsters very much and thought everyone did. He once created a trick photography picture of Dracula next to the girl he was attracted to in school and gave it to her with a note about how much he liked her. He thought the picture was cool and would make her smile, but she didn't agree and showed no interest in him.

While others did not think monsters were great, he and his father absolutely did! They would watch films with Bela Lugosi and Boris Karloff, but Tim's favorite movie was *The Wolf Man*, starring Lon Chaney Jr. Tim was able to please his father with his knowledge of all the monster's strengths and weaknesses. There was something intriguing to Tim about someone who was good and pure of heart by day, but who, by the light of the moon, became vicious and dangerous. Perhaps the boy realized that he had both sides in himself, or perhaps he was subconsciously relating the wolf man to his father's two sides.

When Ken was happy, he was so much fun, and Tim loved laughing at his silliness. He was loving and goofy and just the kind of father a boy would want. Ken would hug his children often and could easily tell them that he loved them. He told horribly corny jokes and loved to have his children scratch his head as they watched television together. Tim loved this side of his father. He also loved his father's ability to impact people. Tim used to watch Ken preach and was amazed at his father's ability to persuade and inspire people. When Tim was in the church pew, all he wanted to be was just like his father. He just could not put the two fathers he knew together. One was gifted, spiritual, fun, and an inspiration. The other was unpredictable, angry, hurtful, and scary. It just didn't make any sense…until that one night.

THE NIGHT THE PLEASER FOUND OUT THE TRUTH

Tim, now twelve years old, had been away at a youth group retreat for the entire weekend and returned to a seemingly empty house. "Hello. Is anyone home?" he asked. No one answered. As he explored the house, he eventually heard sobbing coming from his parents' bedroom. There, again in the dark, was his father sobbing like a child.

"Dad, what's wrong?" he asked (without attempting to hug him).

His father's only reply was, "Go ask your mother."

Tim eventually found his mother and siblings in his sisters' room, huddled together and crying.

"Mom, what is going on? You've got to tell me."

She was silent for a few moments and then told him, "Your father has had an affair with your Sunday school teacher. It is not his first affair. There have been many." Then she just sobbed.

As Tim attempted to comfort her, he had no idea how their lives were going to change.

THE MOVE

His father was fired from the church, but in those days, information was not easily obtainable, so Ken did not have to confess to his new church about his affair. Back then, it was much easier to escape your past. Ken found another church in a small town in Ohio and went back to preaching. His children loved him and forgave him for the affairs, but it was more difficult for Tim to forgive his father for the way he treated Tim's mother. He only wanted harmony between them, and his gentle soul hated the conflict. The pleaser wanted peace, and his parent's fights were many and often loud. Ken's deep sense of guilt was masked by a fiery anger that he took out on Frances. One night, as they screamed at each other through a closed bedroom door, Tim heard a loud crash and went running to protect his mother. As he opened the door, he saw his father standing over his mother, who was sitting in the remnants of a broken mirror. Ken told him to leave, but he refused. At the young age of thirteen, Tim knew that this had to end. He had to find some way to bring peace; he had to find some solution to make his mother happy again.

THE PLEASER'S ROLE IN THE DECISION TO DIVORCE A SECOND TIME

Frances said many years later that Tim's confession that he was afraid he would end up hating his father was one of the pivotal moments that made her choose to divorce Ken. (This haunted Tim for years afterward—was he responsible for their divorce? He was just thirteen years old!) She had left their father and moved back to Ohio, where she got an apartment in the only place she could afford, a government-subsidized housing complex that she did not realize was surrounded by drug dealers and users. Tim was the first child to join her there. In his eyes, he was now the man of the house and she needed him. She needed a hero. He wondered if he was up to the task.

THE TARGET

High school in their new town in Ohio was difficult. Tim felt even more powerless and depressed. He saw his mother's pain and could not do anything about it. He saw the financial pressures as her waitressing job simply did not bring in enough money, and he was helpless. All of five feet, four inches tall, he walked around his new school with slumped shoulders and eyes facing the ground. This made him a target.

In his first week at his new school, Tim walked out of the lunchroom and was grabbed by five football players who picked him up and sat him down on a radiator. A crowd started forming around them, as passersby could see the potential for entertainment. The biggest bully in the group started screaming at the hero. "There are three things we don't do at this school!" he bellowed. "First, we don't swear."

Tim naively responded, "That's OK. I don't swear."

"Shut up! I'm talking!" the bully responded. "Second, we don't spit!" At this point, the bully and the other four started laughing, going on to cite the third rule. "And we don't sit in spit."

As the huge crowd started howling in laughter, Tim realized that the bullies had spent some time spitting on the radiator before sitting him on it. His jeans were soaked with spit. Tears welled up in his eyes, and he stared at the main bully. In his mind, he wanted to hit him, scream at him, and scream at all of them for their cruelty. However, he was a coward and simply ran away sobbing as the crowd continued to relish the entertainment.

If life had been kinder, this would have been the only such incident, but these types of events became a weekly and sometimes daily ritual. Books were knocked out of Tim's hands in the halls almost daily; he was threatened, pushed around, and thrown in thorn bushes. The variety of cruel acts seemed endless. The bullies had found their plaything, and on each occasion, Tim would simply back down and then cry by himself in the darkness of his room.

He could not bear their torment. He could not bear his own inability to stand up to them. One night, it all seemed too much to take. His mother and siblings were gone. He found his brother's loaded .44 Magnum. Holding the gun to his temple, he could only think of ending the constant pain and humiliation that he felt. It was just too hard to go on. He prayed a quick prayer for forgiveness and then started to pull the trigger.

His finger trembled as he pulled the gun away and dropped his head. His first thought, *I can't do this to my mother*, had stopped him from pulling the trigger.

The second thought affirmed his decision to live. He would not let bullies take God's precious gift of life away from him. They didn't deserve that power. *Maybe it won't always be like this*, he told himself, not knowing just how much his life would change for the better as he grew up. Not knowing that the experience he had just gone through would lead him to help others in the same position. He simply decided that night that if life would not take care of him, he would take care of himself. He never thought of harming himself again.

Despite the bullying, there were bright spots in Tim's high school years. He remembers how special birthdays were, when he and his mother would go out, just the two of them, to any restaurant he wanted. He always picked the Brown Derby and always ordered lobster. Even if Frances could not afford it, she never let on. This was her son's special night.

Another bright spot came when Tim found a best friend at school named Bruce who helped him get through those tough years. Pale and lanky, Bruce knew what it was like to be picked on, so he and Tim understood each other well. They became inseparable for many years and even found work together as janitors. This was a way for Tim to bring in some money to help with the food and clothing needs at home. Bruce had many friends and brought Tim into that circle which, at times, kept some of the bullies away. Tim was nicknamed "the Brain" due to his good grades and diligent school work. This, of course, only worsened the bully experience. Tim knew that he needed to change his life. He needed to do something differently.

THE PLEASER TURNS LIFESAVER

Tim spent a lot of time at Christian church camps in the summers as a camp counselor, and the summer before his junior year in high school, he decided he wanted to become a lifeguard. Later in life, he gained the insight that he was attracted to the job because of the potential for saving lives. Therefore, he took the classes and, upon completion, was certified. This made his father proud because of Ken's inability to swim. He respected the fact that his son did not adopt his fear and in fact became one who could save others who had his same weakness. Tim rarely felt his father's pride in him, but he saw that this accomplishment elevated his status in his father's eyes. He was no longer the weak, gentle boy but rather a young man who had defeated something his father feared. He joyfully realized that he had pleased his father.

The next summer, he applied for and got a job as the sole lifeguard at his favorite camp. He grew six inches over the summer, and something incredible happened—girls liked him! The lifeguard position gained Tim a lot of attention, and as a result, he also gained confidence. In high school, he would strike out when playing baseball. At church camp, he was hitting home runs. In high school, he could barely ask a girl out on a date (and was shot down the few times he mustered the courage to say, "I know you probably don't want to, but do you want to go on a date?"). At camp, with rotating camp helpers every week, the teenage girls were asking him to date them for the week. Later in life, he would realize that this message about your position making you attractive would cause him to wonder if anyone could love him just for who he was, but then, he simply loved the attention and grew in his self-assurance. He learned that accomplishments pleased others and could protect him from the rejection he dreaded.

Tim enjoyed being both a lifeguard and camp counselor. At this time, Tim decided he was going to become a psychologist. (Again, he only knew subconsciously that he was picking another role that saves lives.) When he returned to school the next year, at five foot ten inches, tanned, and more confident, he was not approached by a single bully. No punches were thrown; the simple matter of feeling good about himself kept the bullies away. All of a sudden, life was good, and he was accepted and even liked by many. However, life at home was still difficult.

THE PLEASER CONFRONTS THE CHARMER

Tim would travel to his father's home every other weekend. His father had managed to keep his church even after the divorce, as the parishioners had no idea what had been wrong in his marriage. One Sunday, one of Tim's Sunday school teachers was being overly friendly with him, showering him with praise and hugging him. After the revelation of his father's previous affairs, Tim knew exactly what was going on. He had seen this pattern before. Whenever a married woman from one of the churches inexplicably started fawning over him, it meant that his father was sleeping with her. Soon afterward, he decided to confront his father.

"Dad, this just isn't right." Tim hoped that being confronted by the son who had been taught that such things were wrong would lead his father to look at what he was doing and help him avoid more self-destruction.

However, this time, his father was not sorry. He was furious, and his anger exploded onto his son. "You have no say in my life; I can do whatever I want. You are never to repeat this, and I don't even want to look at you right now." Ken, now enveloped in guilt, turned angry, stormed out, and left Tim in the darkness of the basement.

Tears in his eyes, Tim made the hour drive home to be with his mother. This incident damaged his relationship with his father for many years, as Tim again felt a complete inability to be genuine, stay who he was, and still please his father.

JUDGING THE ADDICTED ONE

School was more bearable now, and soon, Tim would go off to college. He tried to concentrate on the possibilities of life, a gift he had learned from his mother, though he was more of a realist. He was not paying attention on his daily walk home from school as he passed a building in their complex where some drug dealers lived. However, a familiar silhouette drew his attention. He turned the corner to see his youngest sister smoking a joint with some of the neighborhood junkies. Tim (who could judge others harshly) was furious with her and just walked away. His judgment was fast and brutal. He told her later that if she did not tell their mother, he would. She did confess, and Tim felt confident that he had done the right thing.

Many years later, he would question his actions and wonder how their paths would have been different if he had shown a different reaction, if he hadn't acted so self-righteously. He still does not know. He left the family to go to college soon after this and removed himself from the situation both physically and emotionally.

Tim's college years were both fun and challenging. He went into college with a new identity. He was no longer a shy, nerdy boy but rather a confident young man who had developed his emotional intelligence and charm. He had figured out how to please people and that if people were happy with him, he would feel safe and good about himself. He immediately started dating, sometimes having three dates in a weekend. He was no longer afraid of women. His first roommate had been a football player in high school (just like those who used to pick on him), but with his new chameleon-like identity (becoming what others wanted in order to please them), Tim bonded quickly with his new friend. He was now one of the cool guys and started acting like it. The first year was full of fun and adventure, and Tim subconsciously left his old life behind, rarely thinking of the pain his family was going through.

MEETING MARLA

It was in the second semester of his freshman year that Tim met the woman who would change his life. They immediately fell in love with each other. Tim thought she was gorgeous and found that she had a stabilizing effect on his somewhat dramatic emotions. She found him fun and interesting and had a mutual attraction. But the match was not ideal. Subconsciously, Tim was attracted to her reserved nature because it meant that she would never cheat on him as his father cheated on his mother. Marla came from a family who, while moral and kind, were very reserved emotionally. She was uncomfortable with touch and displays of affection, and Tim longed to express his deep feelings and have someone who would do the same. Eventually, this difference in expressiveness became an obstacle Tim could not overcome, and he broke up with her at the beginning of his sophomore year.

He was pleased with his decision and started dating again, and everything was good until Marla started dating a football player. At some point, as his jealousy grew, Tim realized his mistake and pursued Marla again, only to be rejected just as he had rejected her. While his outside demeanor was confident, his internal life was still full of insecurity, shame, and a deep fear of rejection, so he did not take her choosing another over him well. He became more impulsive and immature, and eventually, the "inner nerd" returned in full force. Tim's football-playing roommate and others now saw who he really was, and they did not like it. They decided to remove him from their group. His own behavior resulted in the very thing he feared—rejection.

THE LETTER

Tim would travel home to see his family only on the holidays. They seemed to be doing better. His mother was now dating the man who would eventually become his stepfather. He seemed like a nice person and was very generous. The first time Tim met him was at a fancy dinner to which the man was treating the family. He told them to order whatever they wanted on the menu and requested multiple appetizers. Tim thought to himself that he would like to be that person one day, the person who treated others. Having grown up without money, Tim knew how much it meant to be treated to a special dinner by someone. Tim was so impressed that he told everyone around him about this special meal and his hopes that this man would take good care of his mother.

Two weeks later, he was surprised to get a letter from this man, stating how he admired Tim and wanted to give him ten thousand dollars to use as he wanted. Tim was in shock. He was attending college on grants and loans and was working twenty hours a week in order to get by. This money could change everything. He tried to call his benefactor to thank him for the incredible gift but found out he was on a business trip for a week. A week later, Tim was about to call him to share how he planned to buy a car with the money and how this man's act of kindness meant so much to him. Just before he picked up the phone, one of Tim's friends called him, laughing, and said, "Did you get my letter?" revealing that he had sent it to Tim as a joke. The "friend" found it hilarious that Tim had fallen for the gag. Disappointed and betrayed, Tim tore up the letter and remembered at that moment the lesson he learned years before—no one would ever take care of him. If he was going to be successful in life, he would have to do it himself. Self-protection became a major theme for Tim. Protect by pleasing others and protect by never expecting others to take care of you.

MARRYING INTO STABILITY

Despite his deep hurt and feelings of rejection, Tim had learned how to adapt. He picked himself up, made new friends, and started dating other women. Eventually, Marla broke up with the football player, and she and Tim started dating again. They married the summer after his junior year in college, both looking forward to years of happiness together. There would instead be years of difficulty as Tim continued to long for her affection, touch, and adoration. His need for attention seemed to be a bottomless pit. He wanted Marla to be constantly pleased with him and would get very upset when she was disappointed in things he said or did.

Marla worked as a legal secretary to put Tim through graduate school. These were tough times as they were both stressed and growing further and further apart in their interests and thinking. They even separated briefly (although they never told their families) but were always drawn back together. Tim's wounds from his past would often cause him to react emotionally and out of insecurity. Deep down, he was afraid she would leave him, and out of his fear, he pushed her away. At least this way, he could control it.

Nevertheless, Marla was stable and loyal and would always forgive Tim for his weaknesses, dramatic emotions, and mistakes. In return, he would accept her for her lack of expressiveness and emotional connection as he saw glimpses of it developing and growing. Through many difficult times, tense years, and major hurts, they grew to love each other more deeply and more unconditionally. They were always imperfect in their love, but they kept trying to grow and learn how to love each other unselfishly.

WHEN THE PLEASER WAS LOVED BY THE CHARMER

One blessing during his early marriage years (that later became a curse) came in the form of Tim's relationship with his father. Years earlier, Ken had remarried, but now Tim suspected that he was cheating on his new wife. A female parishioner was inexplicably showing attention to Tim, and he knew this pattern very well. Tim still could not sit back and watch his father's damaging choices. He confronted his father more gently this time, asking him, "Dad, are you cheating on your wife again?"

Ken denied his behavior at first but then came back a few weeks later and confessed to his son. "I'm sorry that I lied to you. I have been cheating on your stepmom. Don't you want your father to be happy? I need you to support me in this and be my confidant."

His father's new attitude shocked Tim. The father who had never had much use for him now wanted him as a friend and confidant. Tim chose not to question his father's decision again. He betrayed all he believed in for the privilege of becoming his father's secret partner. He had always wanted the fallen pastor's love, and now he had a way to get it, a way to finally please his father. For years, Tim kept his father's terrible secret, even becoming the person his father talked to about his feelings and love for this other woman. "I'm my father's best friend" was all that Tim could see.

DEALING WITH THE CHARMER'S CANCER

Tim traveled back frequently to see his father during the two years he struggled with cancer. He would counsel his dad, place cool washcloths on his forehead, and do anything he could do to ease his pain. He watched as his larger-than-life, charming father turned into a skeleton. Ken nearly died multiple times, and on one such occasion, he called Tim to be by his side.

"Son, I need you to do something for me," he said.

Tim responded, "Dad, you know I will do anything for you. Just name it." He never suspected that his father's request was for Tim to break up with Ken's latest girlfriend.

"She keeps visiting me in the hospital, and your stepmother is getting suspicious. I need you to tell her that I love her, but that we are over."

What could Tim say to his best friend and the man he wanted to please? "Of course I'll do it for you."

As he sat in the girlfriend's house, holding her while she sobbed and talked about her love for his father, the twenty-three-year-old pleaser could barely wrap his mind around the bizarre experience. "I am comforting a woman twice my age who is having an affair with my dying father that no one knows about. You have got to be kidding me!" However, Tim had dreamed of earning his father's respect, and this was a pivotal moment to come through for his father. Be in on the secret. Betray your integrity. Please others any way you can. This was a horrible and dangerous lesson for Tim. Pleasing protected his soft soul from rejection but removed him from who he was and who he wanted to be.

In his two years of struggling with cancer, Ken, once weighing more than two hundred pounds, eventually fell to only eighty pounds. His shriveled body looked years beyond fifty-two. He had once drawn the desire of many women, but now he relied on his second wife to clean him and help him dress. Unlike in his younger years, Ken's anger was infrequent, even though he struggled with constant pain. He was more gentle, loyal, and loving. He had about a year left to live more like the man he wanted to be, a man focused on pleasing God as best he could. He fought his cancer hard, and there were many ugly moments, as he would often imagine bugs and demons around him due to the large doses of morphine. He would get bedsores and also had to have a colostomy. Tim would tend to him whenever he was visiting, putting lotion on his badly chapped lips or whispering comforting words of peace and love. While horrible and painful, these days were also blessings for Tim, as he knew without any doubt that he had forgiven his father. He loved his father with all of his heart, and he knew for sure that his father loved him.

Tim was back at graduate school studying clinical psychology and running his dissertation experiment when he got the call. "Your father is dead." Tim barely remembers the six-hour drive to get to the hospital where his father had been dying over the last many months, but he remembers in vivid detail his arrival. A hearse was leaving the parking lot of the hospital, and Tim just knew that his father's cold body was in that car. He swerved in front of the hearse and jumped out of his car.

"You have my dad in there. I have to see him," he said, tears streaming down his face.

The driver argued with him for a while, but by this time in his life, Tim was strong and very persuasive; he had taken on some of the gifts of the charmer. As the driver opened the door, Tim saw his father, eyes and mouth open with a look of terror on his pale, gaunt face, in a plastic bag. To Tim, it looked like his father had suffocated in that bag, desperately clawing to get out. That image would haunt Tim for years. He would have nightmares of his father in the distance, and he would run to catch up with him, but his father would keep moving away, or when he touched him, Ken had no substance. He was intangible.

CHAPTER 10

ARE YOU A PLEASER?

UNDERSTANDING THE PLEASER

THE PLEASING SOFT SOUL CAN TAKE MANY FORMS. UNLIKE FIGHTERS, PLEASERS hate conflict and see it as the last resort to fix a situation. Pleasers focus on making others happy and bringing peace to their lives. Pleasers hate to see others suffering, unhappy, or in danger. They dislike people being bullied or taken advantage of by others. They want to have a positive impact on the world and want to save others from negative circumstances, poor relationships, difficult challenges, etc. They often strive for success in fields that affect or save lives. This makes them feel loved and appreciated by others, which can be an almost insatiable quest.

The shadow side of the Pleaser comes in many forms. At times, Pleasers get addicted to the positive attention they get from others. They will ignore their own needs in the pursuit of making others happy but can later become bitter about this and feel like victims. Also, when Pleasers fail and are rejected or beaten up by the harsh world, they can forget the noble calling to help others and focus rather on protecting themselves and lack genuineness in their pleasing of others. They daydream of being loved by everyone and often have the belief that this goal is achievable if they are just good enough. In other archetypal literature, the Pleaser is also referred to as the lover, the intimate, the sensualist, and the team-builder.

Major Tendencies

Pleasers like to help people. If you are the type of person who can easily spot needs in others and feels driven to help them, you might be a Pleaser soft soul. Pleasers feel others' pain deeply and want to save them from their difficulties. They want to help others, and they find great comfort in aiding others physically, financially, and emotionally. Pleasers want peace and harmony.

The Positive Aspects

The intentions of the Pleaser are noble. Pleasers want others to be happy. Pleasers can be very capable and successful if their profession is one that gives them an avenue to help others feel better or reach their goals. By helping people do this, they receive the appreciation and love they desire. At their best, they freely give to others and are willing to put aside their own needs for other people in need. They want others to feel loved.

The Shadow Side

Pleasers, while often noble in intent, may have a shadow side of longing for others' adoration. At their worst, they fall into an insatiable need to be loved and forget the nobility of being a true help to others. They can often feel overly responsible and can drive themselves intensely to create the means and time to help others. Pleasing can become a drug for them, and displeasing someone becomes a horrible life event. Pleasers, when overstepping their role, start feeling the responsibility of saving others in places where it is not their job. Pleasers can be very hard on themselves and can be devastated by any signs of rejection.

Strategies for Integrating Your Soft Soul While Honoring Your Pleasing Tendencies

- If you are a Pleaser, it is better and more appropriate to see yourself as a helper of others rather than a savior. Use your abilities and success to aid others, but do not burden yourself with needing to save them or believe it is truly in your power to make them happy.

- Avoid the sense of failing if the person you are helping is not pleased by you. First, some people will be miserable no matter what you do to help them. Second, there are situations that you can make better with support but that you can never completely heal or change. Think about the expectations you have of yourself. Would you have those same expectations of a friend you love? If so, keep them. If not, face the fact that you do not get special rules. To put rules on yourself that you would not put on others is, in a way, arrogant.

- If you start feeling angry about the number of people that you feel you need to please or the amount of pleasing you are doing for a specific person, just remember that it is *your* choice. There is no reason you have to please or help them. It is OK to say no when you need to. If you do say yes, make sure you are doing so freely, without expectation. There is no burden in it if you *want* to do it.

- Accept the reality that you can't please everyone all the time. Sometimes, it is not appropriate to please the other person if they need to be confronted about unethical or wrong behavior. Don't betray your sense of identity and morals for the temporary "fix" of someone's approval, love, or peace in the relationship. Focus on staying centered on your values and character so you can stay pleasing to yourself.

- Finally, remember that it is OK to give people the gift of disappointment. Many times, we try to please in order to keep the other person from feeling disappointed, but disappointment is just the natural emotion that someone feels when they don't get something they want. There is absolutely nothing wrong with someone feeling disappointed if you didn't do something they wanted you to do (unless, of course, they are attacking you for it). Allow them to feel that way, and don't try to stop them from feeling what is just a normal emotion for the situation.

CHAPTER 11

SOFT SOULS WHO ARE POOR IN SPIRIT

The Story of an Invisible One

THE INVISIBLE ONE

Jamie was not with her father when cancer stole his last breath. She wondered what he was thinking about before his eyes closed for the last time. Did he see the face of the first man he baptized into a new life in Jesus Christ? Did he see the woman healed from blindness after he and his elders prayed for her? Were his successes as a beloved pastor prominent in his final thoughts, or was there something else that haunted him in those moments? Did he see the faces of his many lovers or that of Frances, who had placed all her dreams in his hands, trusting him, only to be repeatedly betrayed? Did he see her or his children, sobbing and frightened at his own hand, cowering below this man so much bigger than they were?

He was no longer that man. Cancer had humbled him as it does all men. Had the memories of his failures left him? Did he wonder if God was waiting to judge him, if God would see all the good he had tried to do, or would He see him as simply the bad seed of a criminal father? Jamie wondered if her father was afraid when he took his last breath.

She hated that she could not be with him as he left this earth, but she had a terrible choice to make, and in the end, she had chosen to leave him. Jamie had made a promise when she was nine, a vow that she would protect children. That vow meant that her needs, desires, and goals had to be put aside. She would choose protecting children over love, over a career, over everything she had dreamed of as a young girl. Her desires had to fade away, disappear, and become invisible. But her mission of protecting children from the harm of the world was impossible to fully achieve, and in her eyes, when others were hurt by the world, it was her fault. She should have known better; she should have seen it coming; she should have saved them! Despite her best efforts, she felt inadequate for the task, disqualified for the objective. She felt poor in spirit, knowing that she needed to rely on more than just her own inadequate abilities. The task was just too big.

THE INVISIBLE ONE'S BEGINNINGS

Some soft souls are born that way, and some develop due to their experiences with the harsh world. Jamie was the first girl born to Ken and Frances. She wasn't born a particularly soft soul and actually came into the world a crusader in spirit. Joan of Arc, they called her in her younger years, but Joan of Arc's spirit had been burned in flames of guilt, failure, and fear. Jamie had fought all of her life for her family. She somehow believed that if she fought hard enough, she could repair the damage that abuse and adultery had brought upon them all. As a child, she longed to be her mother and siblings' fortress, but she was small, skinny, and weak. She had even been unable to protect herself.

The memory that haunted her played frequently in her mind. She could hear the sound of her father's footsteps coming down the stairs. She so hated that sound. What had she done? Oh yes, she remembered; she had called her brother a cheater during a board game. She had not realized her father was home, but she knew as soon as she heard his feet pounding down the basement stairs that she had crossed a line from which she could not retreat. She held her body as still as possible and waited. A strong, brutal hand reached into her hair, yanking her off her bottom. Her scalp burned as his hand clenched tighter. She began to cry, which only made him angrier. He screamed at her as he dragged her up the stairs and down the hall to her room. Her feet fell from beneath her, and he tossed her small body into the wall. She slid to the ground as his hands slapped her repeatedly.

If it was only a beating, she could have easily forgotten it. It was what he did next that had always haunted her. That same man who had just beaten her to the floor fell into a frail heap and began to sob. Ken's head shook back and forth. "If you would just be good," he cried, "I would never have to do this."

She remembered the pain in her lower back and leg as she crawled on her hands and knees across the floor and pleaded with him for his forgiveness. "I'm sorry, Daddy. I'm sorry. I'll do better."

He left her sitting there in the middle of the room, unable to stand up. She couldn't even hate him. He had not even left her that. She blamed herself for failing him. She had loved him despite his failures. He seemed to understand her, the part of her that longed to create, to write, to make movies, to live in a made-up world. All of that came from her father. She was more like him than her mother, she thought. She wanted him to love her, to be proud of who she was.

Later that night as she lay in her bed, the pain kept her from sleep, and the shame filled her up. Then the anger came. She had to keep this a secret. When her mother came home from work, Jamie smiled and acted as if everything was fine. She was afraid of what he would do if she told her mother. She could not bear to see her mother hurt. She forced herself not to cry anymore. She felt so alone.

"I swear," she said, "when I grow up, I will never, ever let any of the kids in my family feel this way. When I grow up, nobody will hurt the children I love. No child will feel this lonely."

She was only nine, but it was a vow she was destined to keep in a way that would dramatically shape her life as an adult.

THE INVISIBLE ONE'S PLACE IN THE FAMILY

She was the third child of Ken and Frances, an unenviable place for any offspring, but she felt hers was particularly unenviable. Her delivery closely followed the birth of the child of their mother's heart, Tim. He was destined to fill the void left by his father's failures. Although Jamie had fulfilled her mother's dream of having a little girl, she was neither infinitely childlike nor cuddly, qualities her infant sister, born just twenty-two months later, oozed. Christi, with the soft, chubby cheeks, tiny freckles, and shy, childish voice, quickly stole everyone's hearts. They had not known that the same sweet, meek girl would break all of their hearts.

Jamie loved her little sister. Her mother would smile as she walked past their room at night and caught the elder daughter kissing Christi's cheeks. She loved those cheeks. They were so smooth and had not lost their baby chubbiness or softness. Even then, Jamie thought, *I have to protect her. She needs me.*

It was not long until they all needed a protector. The next two years brought horrible, fearful changes. Their father's rages grew worse as he battled the horrible guilt born of living two lives, and his hatred of himself fueled the family's rapid descent into destruction. Jamie had a gift for knowing people's spirits and for sensing subtle changes. She used this awareness to try to guide Christi through the chaos. She knew when to hold her baby sister in her place to prevent her from being punished harder for running away. She knew when it was safe to grab her sister's tiny hand and escape to their room. There, huddled in the corner behind the dresser, she would hold her sister's small hand and feel it tremble inside her own. Christi's hands would tremble and shake the rest of her life, and her sister would hold them often through the years. She wanted to be her hero, to save her sister from this veiled nightmare, but she was only seven and ill-equipped to handle the fears of a five-year-old who could hear her father beating the walls as he went up the hall. She didn't have the skills, the talents, or the words that her older brother Tim possessed.

Tim was two years her senior, all of nine years old. He was the only one with blond hair and blue eyes, well read in comic books, talented, and above all, funny. As soon as he could safely make it, he would sneak into their room, and their favorite comedy show would begin. This towheaded, brainy boy quickly transformed into "Dr. Suzuki," a farsighted doctor who could not tell an ear from a nose or a foot from an arm. He was always checking heartbeats in the head and headaches in the feet of various stuffed animals and the youngest sister's beloved Raggedy Ann. He would then announce that the animal had come down with some strange ailment, which of course sounded even funnier in his ridiculously bad Asian accent. They would find themselves laughing aloud in the midst of their fears. Yes, Tim was their hero, and Jamie would spend her whole life wishing that she had her older brother's ability to drive away the darkness and miraculously conjure joy in the most joyless times.

THE INVISIBLE ONE AND THE FIGHTER

Their oldest brother was another matter completely. Jamie and Paul fought like cats and dogs. Paul had earned his title of fighter without trying. From forcing Tim into drinking shaving lotion to bravely taking on the neighborhood bullies, he never stepped down. Initially, Jamie's will was as strong as Paul's when it came to challenging his bullying. They butted heads at every instant. It didn't help that Christi, the sister they both adored, used that adoration to her advantage. She loved to take a swipe at her older sister and then run to the eldest brother for protection. Christi knew her sister well enough to know that Jamie would fight to prove she had been wrong, which would make Paul even madder, and he would pummel Jamie harder. Yet Jamie loved him! That did not keep him from telling her to shut up every time she opened her mouth in an attempt to sing like him. It didn't keep her from telling on him to their parents even when Tim provoked him. Despite their differences, they were family, and family meant everything to them. They fought constantly but would have fought for one another into eternity.

NOT THE USUAL GIRL

Jamie's mother had always wanted a girl, but the eldest daughter had a different take on girlhood than her mother. While she loved her Barbie dolls and occasionally dressing up, Jamie was not into cuddling and girlie things. She was completely disorganized, and she felt that her mother, unaware that Jamie had attention-deficit disorder (something not discovered until she was an adult), found it frustrating to understand why she was not more like her. Frances kept a beautiful house, ran on an organized but flexible schedule, and rarely lost things. Jamie, on the other hand, was scatter-brained. She was always forgetting her lunch, losing her glasses, or fading off into another world while her mother struggled for her attention. Her mother had no idea of the magical worlds her daughter was creating in her mind—the characters, the stories, the adventures that helped her daughter escape. She would hide in this world, often becoming even more invisible to the outside world. Jamie and her mother loved each other greatly, but they were night and day, sand and sea. Yes, they loved each other, but they did not "get" each other.

Christi, on the other hand, though she was somewhat of a tomboy in very feminine fashion, constantly sought being touched, being held, being the center of someone's world. Frances relished the adoration of this little meek girl. She did not love Christi more, but there was a special connection there, a camaraderie of souls she did not share with Jamie.

It became the pattern of Jamie's life. She fought to be a hero, failed to deliver, came short of her target. She was not the best fighter, not very heroic, nor the fragile, easily shattered, meek girl who had to be handled with care. She had no place in life. She felt that she was born between the child of their mother's heart and the adorable and needy youngest child. Even outside of the family, she felt invisible. The teachers raved over her brilliant older brother Tim and her little sister was a magnet for attention. Jamie began to fade away in the shadows of her siblings.

NIGHTMARES COME

Jamie was just eleven the night it happened. Her father had been in a rage all day, and he had gone into the room with her mother. Jamie heard her mother begin to scream, "Stop it! Don't touch me! Leave me alone! Stop! Oh please, stop!" It lasted only about fifteen minutes, and then there was silence. In her child's heart, she feared the silence meant he had killed her.

Jamie wanted to grab something and run in there and beat him off her, but she was terrified she would find her mother in a pool of blood. She lay next to the window, running her fingers on the screen until they almost bled, unable to move, hating herself for not getting up. She fell asleep several hours later.

As she dreamed, the ground opened up, and she saw her mother's body down in the dirt. She began to scream, but there was no sound. Her father stepped up behind her, and his hand gently touched her back. He looked so sorry, but his hand pushed on her spine harder and then harder, and she found herself falling. She could feel her mother's body in the dirt below her, and she struggled to grab her and fight her way out of the dirt. The dirt fell into her eyes and onto her face. Then her father lifted the shovel and poured a pile of dirt into her mouth. She could not breathe. Everything went black.

Jamie sat up in her bed, gasping for air. It was morning, and she ran into her mother's room. Her mother was not there. She frantically searched the house. Her mother was in the kitchen. She almost fell to her knees when she saw that she was OK. Her father walked by and looked at her. *I hate men*, Jamie thought. But she didn't hate men; she feared them. Jamie feared the destruction she had seen them bring upon the women in their lives, destruction from which a soul struggles to recover. She would never be one of those women, she swore to herself. She would be hard if she had to. She was not ever going to be hurt like that. If needed, she would hide from this potential pain.

The second time her parents divorced, she knew that it would be forever. She was relieved.

DREAMS OF BEING VISIBLE

As a teenager, Jamie dreamed of being a writer and an actress. One is rarely invisible if they are writing a bestseller that everyone loves or standing in front of an audience of hundreds. Her first audition came in high school, and hurrying to get to the school, she fell in a patch of mud and ice. She arrived covered with dirt. No one seemed to even notice. She auditioned for a teacher who talked to another student throughout her audition. Jamie limped home, knowing she was invisible on that stage, and he would never cast her.

Their mother had gone to bed early. Frances was in pain. She had taken a job as a waitress, despite the fact that it was physically difficult on her. The job allowed her to be home early so her children could be supervised. That evening, however, Christi, now in her early teens, came in the house late, and Jamie knew instantly that she had been drinking. Christi threw her arms around her sister and told her how sorry she was and how much she loved her. It was obvious she was drunk. Jamie helped Christi get her boots off and get ready for bed.

The uncontrolled vomiting began shortly after that. As Jamie got down on her knees to scrub the couch cushions, she felt nauseated. It smelled like digested food, liquor, and cigarettes. Jamie cursed herself for not leaving it there and making her sister clean it up, but Frances would be so upset. She had so few nice things left and no money for anything new. She loved that L-shaped couch. It was symbolic of the short-lived peace they had after her divorce from Ken. Frances and her three younger children would all crawl onto the couch together, watch television, and just "be." Yes, Frances would be so upset if she woke up and found her family's haven covered in alcohol-laden vomit.

Jamie held her breath and scraped the mess from the cushion. As she looked at her baby sister, now passed out on the other side of the couch, she wanted to hate her. It was the start of a pattern for most of her life that she would take care of others, and her own desires and dreams would fade into the background.

She had wanted to hate her for years. Christi had changed from that innocent little girl she used to be; she could now be so cruel. She knew all the fragile places inside of Jamie and had no trouble exposing them when thcy were fighting. Jamie sometimes wished she could say the things that would tear Christi apart inside the way she always tore her. The image of that gentle little girl she had been was on her sleeping face now. She still had the chubby cheeks that Jamie had kissed so often as a girl. Asleep, Christi looked so fragile and lost.

Yes, Jamie wanted to hate her; she begged her own soul to harden up and let her hate Christi. Hatred never came, but anger grew, and soon, it was consuming. Her anger grew toward all the people who really meant something to her. Part of her blamed Frances. If her mother would just see what was going on and take control, Jamie would be free. She could let go and live her own life. She blamed Tim and was immediately overwhelmed with guilt. How she missed him. He was the one person with whom she had never felt invisible. When he left for college, her hope left with him. Tim no longer stepped in and took care of things. He no longer protected them. He had left her to take care of it all, and now she was all alone. How could she be angry with him? Tim had done so much for her. He had truly been her hero. She prayed he would come home soon, but when he did, he never stayed for long.

Living in the shadow of those who were more successful, less emotion-prone, or more violently emotional, those stronger or needier, those better or more rebellious, Jamie had almost faded away. She would have all but disappeared had God not gifted her with an amazing imagination. She survived by making herself visible in an invisible world. This was a world of dreams and fantasies written in her stories and played out in her room. Through the years, Jamie had been Batgirl, Wonder Woman, the first female captain of a starship, the missionary heroine of the Christian romance novels she read, the prosecuting attorney who put child abusers away, and the Shakespearean actress accepting the Oscar. In her fantasies, in her stories, in her plays, she was someone significant, and her life had meaning.

GOING TO COLLEGE

The iconic actress sat in the middle of the standing-room-only theater of the University of North Carolina—Wilmington, draped across a hard metal chair with one leg up on another chair. She stared at Jamie as she meekly snuck into drama class, two minutes late. Jamie had been unable to find the theater arts building. All of the students sat wide-eyed and silent as they gazed at the formidable figure before them. Her gray hair curled around an aged but regal face with a strong jaw. The actress's face had been worn by years of disappointment soothed by alcohol, but even though she was in her late sixties, she had none of the frailty of an elderly person. Her body was sturdy, and her voice was commanding. Everything about the actress was strong, intense, and passionate. Jamie was mesmerized, and her fascination with her teacher continued until the end of the semester.

As the class was coming into its last couple of weeks, students were assigned the task of re-creating a beloved object without actually bringing the object with them to class. Jamie's classmates had acted out everything from pictures of lost loved ones to sports equipment that reminded them of times with their fathers. The iconic actress, Jean Muir, had been particularly vocal about the performances, what emotions they evoked, where they succeeded, and where they failed.

It was now Jamie's turn. She sat down on the stage and began to cuddle the invisible object, to touch its arms, to stroke its face. When she finished, she looked to her professor for a response. Jean had an odd expression, something Jamie had not seen on her. Jean choked a little as she spoke. "This object is more than just an object of memory to you. It has a more significant place. That's all I want to say right now, but if you want to hear more of my thoughts, you can come by my office."

Neither age nor all the hardships of life had been able to steal the beauty of the iconic actress's expressive blue eyes. Her soul lived in them, and the power of her emotions, whatever they were, struck people hard when she looked at them. As she looked at Jamie, there was a softness that had not been revealed. Her beautiful eyes filled with tears.

Jamie took a seat in Jean's office, and Jean's faithful dog plopped its head on Jamie's lap. Jean smiled at her. "I didn't want to say what I had to say there in that room, but I could see that object, that doll of yours, and I wanted to cry." She pulled in a deep breath. "Because that doll is the place you have gone more than to any human being for comfort."

Jamie took in a staggered breath as if she had never breathed before, and before she could stop it, her life poured out of her mouth. She spoke about hiding in closets under dirty laundry in hopes of not being found by her angry father and about her mother confiding in her the sexual abuse her mother had endured at her father's hands. She mourned aloud all of the fears and secrets she had contained so long. All of it poured out like pus from a deep, infected wound.

Finally, she told Jean about that big rag doll. Jamie had loved it so, because when her imagination had not been enough by itself, she would put it behind her and wrap its arms around her body. She would close her eyes and imagine that someone loved her, that he held her and comforted her, and he would never cheat on her, never abandon her or disgrace her in any way. In her own damaged and broken soul, she created the perfect man. His name was Raggedy Andy.

For the first time, Jamie was not thinking just about her mother's pain or her sister's. She felt visible. Yet when Jean left the college to pursue other adventures, Jamie felt alone again. She had tried dating but found the only thing valued by the men she met was her body, and she had wanted to be valued for her intelligence, her creativity, and her loving soul. Her mother and stepfather were often away. She was living with her sister in a constant state of fear. She couldn't speak, couldn't sleep, and couldn't breathe without somehow setting Christi off. They were just too different.

She could have left her family. Jean had offered to take Jamie with her when she left, to help her pursue a career in acting. Was it fear that kept Jamie from leaving them, fear of what would happen to them, or fear that she would fail and come back to them carrying more shame than she already had to bear? She did not know, but she declined Jean's offer, and she would look back at that moment many times in her life and wonder what would have been.

Jamie was not book brilliant like her older brother, though she was extremely intelligent, nor did she have her sister's charms, but she was creative. She longed to create. She was driven to it. Hers was the soul of an invisible one.

THE DOCTOR WAS WRONG

Her hand trembled as she found the lump in the top of her breast that had been biopsied the year before. It had grown ten times from its original size.

The same doctor who did her biopsy did not look Jamie in the eyes when she and her mother came to his office the next week. In fact, he leaned against the wall as if the weight of a million deaths lay on his shoulders.

"I am so sorry," he said and struggled to continue. "You do have cancer."

Jamie heard her mother suck in her breath. "What?" was the only word she could get out of her mouth. Her mother began to weep.

"What do we do?" one of them managed to ask.

"I talked to a group of experts in this type of cancer, and they highly recommend a mastectomy."

Jamie, all of twenty-two years old, barely heard those words. Her own words that she had spoken a year before haunted her. She had sat in a plastic surgeon's office with her sister, who had been hit in the eye playing coed softball. There were two women talking about their mastectomies and their breast implants and how they had ruptured. At the time, Jamie thought, *I would rather be dead.*

She prayed now that God had not heard her. She would rather be alive, even if it meant taking her breast. They could take it all. She just wanted to live. She didn't want to put her mother through that. She didn't want to leave the most precious new person in her life, the baby girl her sister had just brought into the world.

SOFT SOULS ARE SOMETIMES THE STRONGEST

The people in her theater group had pegged her as weak, but Jamie still held to the beliefs her parents had taught her. She was emotionally fragile and childlike in their eyes. They did not know her, and in the battle ahead to recover from the physical devastation of her cancer, she would prove just how wrong they were. She didn't cry or cower. She held strong to the Jesus she had accepted as a child. Her faith had been something both her mother and father had given her—their greatest gift to her.

How could her father, the same person who gave her faith, have robbed her of so much of her spirit? When he had received news of his daughter's diagnosis, Ken sequestered himself for days. She was later told he had offered God a bargain—her life for his. Upon hearing this, Jamie melted. She thought that perhaps he had changed his ways and was more sensitive and caring about others' needs. Later, they sat in the plastic surgeon's office and barely spoke. Finally, Ken set down his magazine and said, "Well, at least you're going to have plastic surgery. I am counseling a couple right now who are going through this, and the wife is refusing to get reconstruction. Of course, her husband wants nothing to do with her." Ken said it as if it made perfect sense to him, and then he added, "I keep telling her that she has an obligation to her husband, but she won't listen."

Jamie stared at her father in shock. This was the paradox of him. On the one hand, he was willing to trade his life for her life. What an incredible, loving dad! On the other hand, he could be so insensitive and, in her mind, hateful toward women. The abuse he suffered emotionally at the hands of his mother had damaged him. Jamie had fought hard to understand and forgive her father for his weaknesses, but as a pastor, to humiliate and badger this poor woman and side with her husband was just too cruel.

Something changed in Jamie's soul as she looked at him sitting there. It was not that she did not still love him; he was her father. However, for the first time, instead of being ashamed that she was not good enough to be his daughter, she felt ashamed that he was her dad.

Jamie lay in her hospital bed, knowing that after the next morning, her life would be different, but she refused to yield to fear. Her spirit was filled with peace in the midst of the tragedy, and she started to sing. She rarely sang in front of others, but that night, she could not help herself. She and her mother, who sat at her bedside that night and for many nights to come, began to sing praises. No matter what happened to her, even if she died, God was in control, and that was good enough for Jamie.

She would wake from her surgery to see her siblings gathered about her bed. Her mother held her hand, and tears fell. They all looked so sad. She hated causing them another ounce of pain. She would look at the tubes bringing fluids from the clear bag hanging on her IV pole and, in an effort to cheer them, made a joke that the only thing missing was the goldfish. It felt good to hear them laugh.

It was a few hours later that she woke again, groggy and in pain, and found her eldest brother, Paul, standing beside the pole, holding up a bag of goldfish. They had been at odds all their lives, but there he stood, smiling, and she knew he still loved his little sister.

LOSS OF VISIBILITY

Jamie's father had told her how men felt about "mutilated" women. Now she felt even more invisible to them than ever before. Even her closest friend, who was a man, ended their relationship soon after her surgery. There were a few men in her life after that, but none that mattered, none that saw her. She could no longer believe in the version of love her mother had taught her, and yet in her soul, she could not accept the realities of real-life love, how painful it could be and how thoughtless and how apathetic people grew toward one another with time. Jamie grew weary as she looked at the relationships around her. Lovers who once couldn't stand to be apart no longer touched. Romantic moments turned into fights over yard work and shopping addictions. All of the women around her seemed sad and powerless. She couldn't become that, even if it meant being alone.

Jamie sometimes thought, *Aren't you tired of being lonely?* The answer to herself was always the same: *Isn't it better to be lonely alone than to be lonely beside a person you can never reach? Isn't it better to be something to yourself than to live the rest of your life being less to someone else, yet another person for whom you will never be enough?* Afterward, Jamie gave up romantic relationships. She would choose instead to give her love to her family and to people she could love without pain.

As Jamie sat in her home years later, thinking about those words, she had to laugh—those who would never bring her pain! When she was young, she had believed in such fairy tales, but now, she knew better. In 1985, however, a new life came into her world, and she thought loving her would never bring anything but joy.

Jacki was an exquisite beauty even as a baby, a highly precocious and dramatic little girl. As the first grandchild and Christi's daughter, she was spoiled to no end and demanded everyone's attention. She had no humility about her dramatic talents or her beauty, and somehow, from childhood, she appeared to understand that she possessed a highly unique, vibrant, and entrancing personality. It was such fun to watch her twist the world around her finger. Jacki would never be invisible!

Just a few short years later, Jamie was excited as Christi gave birth to another little girl, Sammi. This child was quite the opposite of her older sister. Sammi was exuberantly joyful and content wherever she was. She loved her bed. She loved the playpen. She could sit, sing, and play for hours with barely a fuss. Her angelic face and lovely blond curls surrounded happy eyes with a blissful smile. She spent her whole childhood in roller skates, racing through the house with a grin on her face. Sammi was a truly gentle soul.

THE BOTTLE

Jamie was pleased, and initially, Christi seemed to take quite well to motherhood. However, her marriage was extremely troubled from the start. Her husband's many months at sea left Christi lonely and depressed. Even visits from her mother and Jamie did not fill the void. She seemed to be desperate for time with her friends and began to leave the house and her daughters when her family came to visit. They thought she might be drinking. Christi had always loved to drink a bit, but soon, it became apparent that drinking was not the problem. The full scope of her difficulties would not come to light until Ken's ordeal with cancer.

The call came; their father's cancer had spread. They needed to come to the hospital quickly. The children of Ken and Frances gathered in a circle in the waiting room, offering up prayers for the man they all loved in spite of his weaknesses. All of Ken's children still had a strong belief in God, despite the fact that their father had failed to practice what he preached. As they held one another's hands, Jamie smiled as she took Tim's hand in hers. It had been so long since she had seen him, and she looked at him with a child's eyes. He was still her hero.

Christi's hand trembled in her sister's, and Jamie squeezed it tighter. There was so much pain hidden inside her little sister, and she wished she could just erase it, but she once again found herself feeling helpless. It was sad and quiet in the room, two things Christi's daughter, Jacki, hated.

Bored and frustrated by all of the emotions, she searched for a distraction. Jacki unzipped her infant sister's diaper bag for a toy to play with. Her face looked surprised. She pulled out a large glass bottle with a black label. "Look, beer!" She laughed, interrupting their tearful prayers. It was not beer at all, but a half-empty bottle of Jack Daniel's. It should have registered as a bad omen, but the children of Ken and Frances could not help themselves, and they burst out laughing.

Their father's battle was unbearable for them to watch. The big man with the odd yet funny sense of humor and the unchallenged sense of authority was now a frail eighty pounds. A shriveled-up shell of a man who looked ninety years old though he was in his early fifties lay before them. He screamed in pain at every touch, and yet his heart refused to give in and let him die. They stayed with him for weeks waiting, saying good-bye every day, only to face another day in which they watched him scream and suffer. Finally, Frances came to them and told them that she had to leave. Her new husband had to return home to North Carolina, and everyone would have to come with them. Christi went insane at this news. She screamed and cried. Her mother would have left her there, but Jacki was acting strangely and seemed terrified to leave her mother. She clung to Christi as if she feared her mother would not come back to her.

"She needs you to come with us," Frances told her youngest child.

"I am not leaving Dad," Christi said as she worked to pry Jacki's hands off her.

"Well, I don't know what to do. Look at her," Frances pleaded. "She is your first priority."

Jamie was standing near them, trying to calm the little girl down, when she saw Christi's hands begin to clench Jacki's arms tightly.

"Stop, Mommy! That hurts!" her daughter squealed.

Christi's teeth gritted shut so tight that she shook, and her grasp got even tighter.

The child wailed even harder, and Jamie could not stand by any longer. She grabbed her sister by the arms and squeezed tightly, sternly saying, "Let her go."

Christi glared at her sister as if she could kill her. That moment was the beginning of a battle between the two women that caused them both years of pain and would leave Jamie full of guilt.

VOWS AND CHOICES

As her father lay in a restless sleep in his hospital bed, Jamie tried to deny the sense of powerlessness she felt. She had nothing to give him but prayers, and yet it did not make what she was about to do any easier. She was leaving him. He was suffering and dying, and she was leaving him. In life, there are choices. Some are easy, and some tear at your soul. She had to make a choice to stay at his side or to protect the defenseless young girls. In her mind, she saw herself as a little girl, lying alone on the floor after Ken had beaten her. That day, she would keep the promise she made to protect others, even if it meant leaving him to die.

Jamie didn't know at that moment that Christi held a secret that would soon make her incapable of caring for her own children. She didn't know that Christi would shatter the hearts of her family. She didn't know she would come to love Jacki and Sammi as her own or that losing them would rob her of a part of her soul. She didn't know that her little sister, who would rob her of so much, would also give her the greatest gift of her life. She only knew she had made a vow in the darkness, and she was willing to sacrifice everything to keep it.

Soon, she found out the secret. Her sister, her sweet little innocent sister, was addicted to crack. Christi's addiction to drugs would change Jamie's life forever. Only years later would she realize that by putting all of her heart and soul into caring for and protecting others, the invisible one, the actress, the writer in her would become invisible even to herself.

CHAPTER 12

ARE YOU AN INVISIBLE ONE?

UNDERSTANDING THE INVISIBLE ONE

Invisible Ones comes in many forms. For example, Jamie is, at the deepest level of her soul, an artist (another common archetype). Yet due to her life circumstances, she has sacrificed her artistic side to focus on being the caretaker of children. Invisible Ones often have another of the archetypes as a core of their personality, but they may not express that archetype because of various life experiences. Perhaps they have been hurt too much by life, so they tend to avoid being too integrated into the world. Perhaps their natural personality was not appreciated or nurtured, so they retreat from the full expression of who they are and want to be. Invisible Ones live in an isolated world. Many Invisible Ones live in fear and pull back from others due to their deep sensitivity and vulnerability to getting hurt. While this provides them with temporary protection, it can also leave them lonely and feeling like they don't have a voice or impact. Some will give up their dreams and desires to live a life that seems safe from the hurt of the world. The beautiful thing about Invisible Ones is that they don't take the spotlight. They let others get the credit and attention. Also, sometimes being invisible actually does protect them from harm.

Major Tendencies

Do you feel invisible to others? Are you often ignored or misunderstood? If so, you may be an Invisible One. Invisible Ones fade into the background. They are often not seen as successful in the eyes of the world, and that is because they do their caretaking for others quietly and without fanfare. Unlike others who get the spotlight for their successes or impacts on the world, the Invisible Ones either live in isolation or take care of others in everyday activities and the mundane. Those who are out in the world with others see a need, and Invisible Ones address the need. They can be especially sensitive to the needs of children and those who cannot protect themselves.

The Positive Aspects

Invisible Ones are good souls. If they have been able to overcome the fears that cause isolation, they care for others and want to help them avoid pain and conflict. They care unselfishly and do not seek the spotlight and attention for their help. They help because it is the right thing to do. They often sacrifice their own dreams for the needs of others. Invisible Ones are acutely aware of their need for God.

The Shadow Side

In the extreme, Invisible Ones hide from the world and fail to contribute anything to other human beings. In the more common form, Invisible Ones can focus too much on others' needs and not enough on their own health, success, and dreams. This can be harmful to their sense of self. They can be prone to an intense sense of responsibility and feel guilty about taking care of themselves. Thus, they can become invisible to their own needs. Invisible Ones who have gone through intense trauma in their lives can experience a strong sense of fear. They care so much about others that it terrifies them that the people they care for could be harmed. They feel responsible for them and therefore can be hyperalert to potential dangers that could threaten their loved ones.

Strategies for Integrating Your Soft Soul While Honoring Your Invisible Tendencies

- If you have isolated yourself from the world, be like the person who slowly gets into a cold swimming pool. Put your foot in the pool before diving into the deep end. Build a list of things that scare you that are likely very safe. Tackle the one you fear the least first. Once you master that, do the next one. Keep checking fears off your list until you have addressed each one.

- If you have become invisible to yourself, you need to focus on finding yourself again. The first step is to explore your feelings and thoughts more than you have done in the past. Use the journaling and venting techniques that we will describe in detail in later chapters. Write a psalm to God to fully explore your inner workings. Face your fears—what is holding you back? No longer allow fear to dictate your decisions, but approach difficult situations a step at a time until you rebuild your confidence or sense of peace.

- Recharge often; you have to replace the energy that you are expending helping others. We will discuss ways to do this later in this book.

- Make sure that you have a support system. You need someone who takes care of you. Become visible to yourself again, and discover what gems you have inside that you might have forgotten.

- Avoid resentment when you get lost. It is easy to resent those who keep taking when you have nothing left to give. Draw boundaries with those people in kindness and love, and stick to them, but if you give in, avoid blaming and resenting them, and realize you must work on your own inner strength to stand firm.

- Believe in yourself, even when you don't! This is probably the hardest thing to understand, but we can learn to believe in the soft soul God created in us and in the person we are inside just by accepting that God made us for a special purpose. We were not an accident. If we accept that we are divinely created and that God is in control of where we are going and what we will be, we realize that what we see as failures and frailties are actually God moving us through that plan. If we just trust that He has us in His palm, there is no risk of our life being a complete failure.

CHAPTER 13

SOFT SOULS WHO ARE MEEK

The Story of an Addicted One

THE ADDICTED ONE

Oh God, she thought. *I finally did it. Oh God, I didn't mean it.*

Christi held her eyes closed as tightly as she could. She heard the demons' voices around her and convinced herself if she didn't open her eyes, they would go away. One laughed a demented cackle so malicious that it made her heart race. Another wailed, the despondent, barren cry of a soul lacking hope for any redemption from its torture. Tears welled up in Christi's eyes. *Just don't open your eyes*, she said inside her mind. *Just don't open them.*

So many times before, she had gone too far, but God had always pulled her out. Christi had swallowed multiple bottles of pills, but she had not died. She had begun to think she was invincible, but now she was dead.

She had crossed the line, and God's mercy had worn out. She deserved it, she thought. There was no sin she had not committed, but she still cried out in desperation, "Please, Jesus, please."

Another wail sounded, this one so violent, so piercing, that it startled her, and her eyes involuntarily flew open. In a haze, she could see the outline of a figure outside the door. It was a shriveled-up old man with his wrinkled, naked backside peering out of his hospital gown. He stood screaming in a pool of his own urine. She was not dead. She was back at the state mental hospital. She had walked this road so long, she thought. This had to be the last time. It had to be.

Memories of the last few weeks filled her mind. The argument she had deliberately caused on Christmas Day so that she could leave her family and go to the man she now loved. The way he swore he was the only one who loved her as they smoked the crack that night, the way he had taken her money and left her with that horrid craving that could not be satisfied. Christi had gone into the streets seeking more. She had to avoid the crash. The crashes were so bad. She had to look at herself. Inside, she was still that meek, innocent little girl who cried when her brothers tossed around her Raggedy Ann doll. How could she become this? How had she become someone so against everything she valued and believed? It was too much. Christi needed to drown out this pain.

"I want my meds," she yelled at the door. "I need my meds!"

"Stop yelling," the nurse scolded bitterly.

More images flooded her mind. She could picture herself on her knees, the gun in her face. That was why she thought she was dead. Had it been yesterday or weeks ago? The dealer's hand shook from his fury. He had wasted his time meeting with her. She had no money, and she was trying to barter some cheap jewelry. Did she think he was stupid? If his brother had not talked him out of it, he would have shot her right there. She imagined her children seeing her there in a pool of blood and her mother dying from the grief. Her hands trembled.

Christi's chest muscles clamped around her ribs, and she ran to the door and screamed, "Where are my meds?"

THE ADDICTED ONE'S BEGINNINGS

Christi was the youngest of the family. She was small and thin and had adorable freckles. The rest of the family adored her—she was almost like a doll they all wanted to hold. They doted on her, but it never seemed to be enough for Christi. She was the meekest of children, spoke like a baby with quiet whispers, and needed so much reassuring. Christi would respond dramatically to any teasing, her feelings hurt easily. Most of the time, she held onto Frances's leg like it was a lifeline, rarely being separated from her. She craved her mother's touch and tenderness. Everyone attributed her shy, quiet nature to simply being the baby of the family. None of them could have known the secrets this little one was hiding, the horrific, nightmarish tortures from which they could not protect her. They would never fully learn the hidden truth. Her mind was being damaged, her soul shattered, and no one suspected a thing.

Who had been the perpetrator of such heinous crimes against Christi? The full secret would never be revealed, but there were details, horrifying details, during drunken moments. While drunk, she would talk of memories of a man forcing her into performing oral sex on him when she was only three. She had nightmares and visions of sick moments but could never identify a face, just the feelings of intense, unending shame.

THE START OF SELF-MEDICATION

Her parents' two divorces and the shattering of the family were especially difficult for Christi. In her early teens, she started drinking and smoking marijuana, partly to fit in with individuals in their new government-subsidized housing complex and partly to soothe the pain of her past and present. Even after being caught by Tim and confessing to her mother, she continued to drink and use marijuana, which opened the doorway to other substances. Abuse had made her past a nightmare, but drugs were creating a nightmare of her present too.

In her junior high school, there were three main groups: the popular kids, the brains, and the "grits." The "grits" were the kids on the outside who often shared a disdain for authority and a love for cigarettes, drugs, and alcohol. They were also paradoxically the ones to be the most welcoming to new kids in the school. Feeling rejected by the popular kids and not feeling like she was part of the brains, Christi decided to follow the grits. In this group, she became the center of attention and was now seen as cool. She came out of her shell and developed a quick, wicked mouth, but she still had those cute freckles, which made it adorable when she was being naughty. She had friends and the kind of fame or notoriousness a junior high kid loves to have, and she was in love. She hoped she could bury her pain in the depths of all their adoration.

Christi had adored, almost worshipped, this first man in her life. He was handsome and fun. He told her she was beautiful and reminded her every day of his love for her. She would have followed him anywhere. He was four years older than she was, which made a sexual relationship illegal, and she wasn't ready for that, not after what she had been through, but he swore he loved her enough to wait until she was ready. His words were lies, and Christi bought them completely. One night at his apartment, he brought out the alcohol, and he poured her more and more. She woke up periodically as he raped her, but all she remembered was pain. The next morning, she had almost forgotten what had happened, but then sickness came over her as she realized what he had done to her. When she confronted him, he cried and begged. He was so broken. He could not control himself, he claimed. She forgave him, but the relationship was short-lived after that as she soon found him cheating on her with another girl. She had given her heart to the wrong man.

There were others who followed after this experience, men who tried to hurt her: a friend's father, a rampant alcoholic who grabbed her and touched her in private places as she passed him; an airplane pilot who let her steer the plane only to try to touch her while she did; an employer who took her to his back room. The wolves sensed her vulnerability. Christi was their prey, their innocent lamb.

Christi reacted to their abuse by acting out. She found power in rebellion and comfort in alcohol and pills. She thought she could do whatever she wanted. Her mother would always forgive her; of that, she was sure. She knew her mother loved her no matter what she did. Frances would not be strong enough to stand up against her. For this reason, Christi had been shocked when Frances finally stood up to her and hospitalized her in a locked ward for her addictions. No one was going to cage her though. She was on a path of self-destruction, and she truly thought she could get around them all. At the hospital, she devised an escape plan, the first of many. She crawled on her hands and knees across the floor in front of the nurse's station. A friend waited in the parking lot with a handful of pills. As she slithered like a snake past the unaware nurses, she almost laughed at how clever she was, but the smile faded. She stopped cold as she looked at the pair of shoes approaching her. It was another patient, a man of limited mental capacities. She tried to shush him, but he was unaware of her attempt and called her by name and asked her what she was doing down on the floor. The nurses ran from behind the desk so fast, they almost ran into each other. After that, to discourage her from escaping, they took her clothes, and she spent the rest of her time there with nothing to wear but a hospital gown.

Once she was released, the drive home was uncomfortable for both Christi and Frances. They had been so close, but now there was this gap. Her mother could not understand. She had taught her daughter the difference between right and wrong. How could she continue to make these choices?

Christi explained, "God and the Devil are in this battle, and we are just pawns. I want no part of it."

"You have to choose," her mother told her with all the love she had ever had.

"I won't," Christi answered.

Her mother's heart grieved deeply in that moment.

While Christi had been hospitalized, her mother had met a kind man. They had talked about Christi, and he had cried. They had begun dating and talked about starting a place for girls like Christi.

Christi was happy when she heard. This man could give her what her father never did, she thought. This man could provide her with the life of which she had always dreamed. Soon, he and Christi's mother married, and he moved them to North Carolina, hoping Christi could start anew. Here, the nightmares seemed more distant. Maybe she could forget. Maybe she could allow herself to heal. Her mother seemed happy too. Frances had sacrificed so much for them. Christi knew she had hurt her mother as her father had done. She wanted so much to make her proud and to be good.

There were adjustments for all of them, but beach life seemed to suit Christi. Besides the occasional beach party drunkenness, she was sober and OK with it. She met the man she would marry. It wasn't an easy relationship, but it was a mostly sober one. They were as different as night and day. He was serious and studious; she was fun-loving and social. They tried their best to love each other. They married on the channel under the blue sky with friends and family. A baby girl was born to them not long after. Despite their conflicts in personality, Christi thought she had a chance to be happy.

HER HUSBAND'S JOB

"I got a job!" her young husband announced. Christi was so happy; maybe this would reduce the stress he had felt. They were fighting so much lately. "It's in Greensboro."

Her heart sank. He was taking her away from her family. What she didn't know then was even worse. He would be out at sea, and she would be in Greensboro with not one but two children, all alone. Who would be there for her? For a lamb who needed to follow someone, who needed to be adored, who needed stability, this was a change and transition that she could barely handle.

The move was everything that Christi feared in terms of her relationship with her husband. Her marriage was falling apart, but her little girls were so amazing. She loved playing with them and being their mom. Her daughters had made everything bad in her life bearable to that point. Unfortunately, things would soon change.

The phone rang. It was her father, and he did not sound good. She could hear it in his voice. The cancer was back, and it was worse. She packed up her children and headed to Ohio.

Watching her father's frail body being eaten up by cancer created a sorrow that drove her to dark places. His body was so withered that you could see each bone, and his once-dark hair was graying rapidly. The lump in his arm pushed out the thin skin that covered it, and Christi tried not to look. She had to be with him. She had to make him feel better. She had to tell him she was sorry for where she had failed him, and she desperately needed him to tell her he was sorry for where he had failed her. But that conversation never happened, as Ken asked all of his children to go home so he could be with their stepmother. Perhaps this was his way of setting his children free, but Christi simply saw it as a final rejection from her father.

BACK HOME

When she returned home, Christi went to a neighbor's house where the local women would party. Her friend greeted her with a warm hug, and it felt so good. She was able to trust her. She had been a good friend and understood so many things. The women all sat around the room. Christi's eyes caught the sight of a glass bong on the table. "Try it," her trusted friend encouraged. "You'll love this."

"What is it?" Christi asked, already having decided to try it (they all seemed to feel so good, and she desperately wanted to be out of her pain).

"Oh, it's just a little something like pot." Her friend laughed.

She put the bong to her lips and breathed in. It was like no feeling she had ever had before, and she felt absolutely no pain. She had no idea what that temporary high would cost her. She had again followed the wrong person and the wrong solution for her pain.

THE DEATH OF THE CHARMER

Jamie was waiting for Christi in the stairwell when she came home from a day out with her husband. Jamie took Christi in her arms and told her that their father had died. Christi's knees went out from under her, and she sobbed hysterically, thinking only of her perceived final rejection from her father. She had been so angry with him, and now he was gone. She could never make it right. She could never tell him that she still loved him.

After Ken's death, her drug use got worse. Christi drove to her mother's house, hoping she would get her children there safely despite the Xanax she had taken. Jamie had been ill and hospitalized, and they were all concerned for her health. Christi went to the hospital to visit her sister, but memories of her father overwhelmed her. Jamie lay in the hospital bed as he had, waiting to find out if she had cancer again. Christi could not stand it. Emotions flooded her, and she needed an escape.

The first true sign her family would have of the severity of Christi's addiction was when Frances woke up in the middle of the night to find that Christi had disappeared. Frances could not comprehend what was happening to her life. Her first husband had died, her older daughter was lying in a hospital bed, and now her youngest daughter was gone in the middle of the night with no note and no clue as to what had happened to her. She screamed through the house, hysterically worried for her youngest daughter. She could not sleep the entire night.

Jamie woke up the next morning and found her little sister sobbing by her hospital bed. Her eyes looked strange. Christi told her sister repeatedly that she loved her. Something was wrong, something more than any of them had suspected.

REHAB AND RECOVERY

"I'll lose my children if my husband finds out!" she argued with her mother.

Frances took her hand. "You'll lose your children if you don't stop doing drugs! Go get help while you can, before your husband finds out what is going on."

"You know it is the right thing to do," her brother Tim assured her. His mother had called for his help. She knew his little sister would listen to him.

They were all broken. Finding out that Christi was back on drugs hurt them in a way she had not anticipated, and she cried because of the pain she was causing. She agreed; she would go for help. They were relieved. This nightmare would soon be over, and they would have their addicted one back—or so they thought.

Christi's thirty days were up, and she had seemed to do well. Her mother and stepfather brought her car to her, hugged her, and told her how proud they were of her. They would see her at their house later that afternoon. Her little girls were so excited to see her. They waited at their house; the three-year-old had planned a coming-home party, and both girls were in their cutest outfits. They waited and they waited. Christi never came. Frances and Jamie knew what she had gone to do.

For a year, the family danced the same dance together. Christi would call in the middle of the night and beg for help, Jamie would drive to Crack Town to try to find her, the family would take her to the hospital, and Christi's little girls would wait for her to come back to them. Sometimes, Christi would make it a month, and sometimes, only a few days, but she would always go back to the streets. Christi was jealous as she saw her children becoming closer and closer to her sister, and she and Jamie began to fight over them. Jamie did not trust Christi with her kids, and why should she? She had let her baby daughter fall out of her bed on several occasions, spanked her three-year-old in anger far harder than she should, screamed at both girls, and left them unattended. Jamie had no reason to trust her, and Christi hated her sister for reminding her that she had failed. Christi's husband had warned her that he would not allow her to keep going like this, but she didn't believe him. He would never take her children away from her. He didn't even know how to take care of them.

His threats echoed in her mind as she snuck past him, sleeping on the couch. He had come to see his children. She couldn't bear to be in the house with him. She had loved him so much. He was the love of her life, but she had never been good enough for him and she couldn't bear the idea of being near him. The shame was too much. She snuck past him and opened the door. She did not think about the consequences. She craved an escape, and it was all that mattered in that moment.

THE ADDICTED ONE LOSES HER CHILDREN

Her little girls sobbed and cried, begging for their mother, grandmother, and their aunt as their father buckled them into his car for the two-hour drive to his home. Christi sunk to the porch step, sobbing in her mother's arms. What had she done? He had warned her, but still, she walked out the door. Jamie did not even look at Christi as she passed by with rage in her eyes. Jamie would go with Christi's husband and teach him how to take care of his little girls. She would make sure they were put in a good preschool while he worked. She would be there for them as long as he would let her. Christi's babies looked out the window as he drove away, their hands on the glass, crying for their mommy.

During this time, Jacki and Sammi's father did his best to give them a normal life. Frances and Jamie drove almost four hundred miles every other Friday and back again on Sunday to make sure they were part of their lives and that Jacki and Sammi knew their mother. They taught the girls about God and about His grace and forgiveness. Soon, the girls forgot about all of the painful nights and simply enjoyed whatever time they could spend with their mother during their visits. It was always an occasion when the girls visited. Their mom would take them to fun, cool places. Their aunt would help them put on concerts and make works of art and plays. Just being with their grandmother was a gift to them. They loved her smile, her wisdom, her nonjudgmental spirit. Despite everything, they all had fun together. Often, just days before they arrived, Jamie and Frances would clean the vomit off of Christi from an all-night binge, or bail her out of jail, or be in a panic because she had been gone three days and they had feared they would have to tell her little girls she was found dead in the streets. They protected the girls the best they could from all of this.

THE PRAYER OF THE IDEALIST

One night in the darkness, Frances was crying and praying, and she called out to God, pleading, "God, help my child." That night, a voice spoke to her heart and said, "You mean *our* child." Frances remembered the prayers of her young motherhood, how she had given each of her children back to God, a lesson she had learned from her firstborn's terrible illness. From that night forward, she still mourned but put her daughter in God's hands and slept.

THE SURPRISE

Several years passed. Christi rolled over in her bed and grabbed her morning pills. She wondered how she had found herself in this position again. She had drunk so much the weeks before, she couldn't even remember most of it. Here she lay, knowing she would have to get her white chip at her next Narcotics Anonymous meeting and start all over again. Her body felt woozy. She could tell it was getting weaker every day. She looked in the mirror and hated what she saw, the scar beneath her eye from the wreck that should have killed her, the darkness under her eyes.

Christi felt sad today. She had her pre-op visit with the doctor. She was going to get her tubes tied. Pain shot through her, and it almost brought her to her knees. Corey—the name rang in her ears. He had been the first baby she had lost to drugs. She had given him a name as a way to try to mourn him, to try to make peace with it. She wondered what he looked like in heaven. Would he know her when she arrived? Would he forgive her? She longed for her children, physically ached to hold them. After today, she would never have another child to love.

She felt something else too. She had failed her sister. She had thought many times about having a baby for Jamie to adopt from her. Now that would never happen, although she knew in her heart she never could have given up her baby anyway.

Christi walked into the doctor's office, focused on making sure that she could talk them into pain pills after the surgery. As she waited, she felt sicker and tried to shake away the feeling.

The doctor came in with an odd look. "We won't be doing your surgery. It appears you are pregnant."

Christi should have been frightened about all the drinking she had done. She should have been in a panic at the idea of bringing a child into her violent, drug-filled life, but this was her chance, the chance to finally do things right. She was going to be the mother she had never been. She wanted to be the mother to her children that Frances had been to her, despite all she had lived through. Frances had always put her kids first despite the pain she had suffered. Christi wanted to be that kind of mother. She wanted to put her children above her pain. She checked herself into the hospital immediately. She planned to go off all of the psychiatric medication she had been taking for the baby's health, but within a few days, she was suicidal, and they put her back on a few to maintain her mental health. She could do it this time.

"You need to abort this baby," one of the nurses scolded, shaking her head.

"The doctor already said that!" Christi snapped. "I'm not doing it!"

"You're just being selfish!" another patient chimed in.

Christi, however, did not think she was being selfish. For the first time in a long time, she was doing the right thing. She would give this child a chance. She prayed God would protect him from the drinking she had done in the beginning. She was going to do it this time.

TRIED AND FAILED AGAIN

Christi sat on the floor of the hospital bathroom, trying not to throw up. What had she done? What had she put this poor baby through? She hadn't felt him moving inside her since she left the hospital and took that first hit of crack a few days ago. Where had she gone? She wanted to die. She wanted to die and take her baby with her. Surely, God would let her come to heaven. She had not asked to be an addict.

Frances tried to talk to her through the locked bathroom door; she told her how much she loved her.

How could anyone love me? Christi wondered, but she knew her mother still did. After everything she had done, Frances had never given up hope. She would never give up. It was not in her mother's thoughts that she could abandon her baby.

Christi could also hear her sister shouting at the nurse in the hall to find a way to unlock the bathroom door. She heard Jamie insisting they take her to the psychiatric part of the hospital.

Why can't she mind her own business? Christi thought as she contemplated her choices at that moment.

The nurse got the maintenance crew to force open the door. They grabbed her up from the floor and tied her down so she couldn't hurt herself or her child.

THE GIFT

He was so tiny that they could see his bones through his skin. He looked more like a little alien than a human baby, but they still found him adorable.

Christi held her new son, and she had hope that the tremendous love she felt would somehow stop her cravings for more drugs. She watched Frances hold her new grandson in her arms and rock him. Frances was so natural as a mother, but Christi had never been that way with her babies. She had loved them, but she had found motherhood frightening. He cried so much, her little man. The doctors seemed concerned, though no one could tell her why he cried so often. They came to take him for tests. Christi looked at her sister. Jamie sighed and took hold of the bassinet as they wheeled the baby boy toward the CAT scan. Jamie tried not to look too much at her nephew. She didn't want to feel the pain she had felt with her sister's girls. She didn't want to hurt for him as she did for them. They took his tiny four-and-a-half-pound body and laid it on the bed of the CAT scan machine. He began to scream. It was a horrible scream, a petrified, startling scream.

Jamie wasn't going to love him, she told herself. She wasn't going to love another child ever, she vowed. Then his tiny hands trembled as they took them to strap him down, and he screamed even louder. Jamie put her finger inside his hand and whispered in his ear.

"It's all right, baby. It's all right. I'm here."

They prayed their new little man would come home by Christmas. The doctors had diagnosed him with acid reflux but other than that thought he was fine. On December 23, they received a call to come get him. Social services had released him to the custody of his grandmother and aunt, and they and his grandfather welcomed him and Christi back home. He was dressed all in blue, and his eyes looked all around. He seemed so alert. Maybe he was going to be all right.

Christmas was beautiful. Though Christi slept through much of it, when she was awake, she held her baby in her arms and seemed so content. His sisters had some small twinges of jealousy but quickly fell in love with the tiny alien brother of theirs who their mother had nicknamed "Doodlebug." Life seemed good.

Christi was calm and peaceful after this baby's birth but also tired and unable to stay awake. The time she could care for her son each day dwindled to just a few hours. Frances was trying to take care of this special needs infant on her own, but this time, Jamie didn't jump in to help. She wanted to be hard, to resist love at all costs. Because of this, Jamie was conflicted when the social worker came to visit. She was a kind woman, caring and passionate about her job. Jamie respected her so much. "Are you ready to raise this little boy?" the social worker asked.

Jamie stopped her. "No, my sister is going to pull it together and raise this baby."

The social worker shook her head and said, "You know you are going to end up raising this little boy, and I need to know that you are willing to do that."

Jamie didn't want to say it; she didn't want to commit, didn't want to promise away what little was left of her. Her eyes filled with tears as she thought about his tiny hands, his curious eyes, and his funny smile. He had her birthmark on the side of his little nose. "I am. Yes, absolutely, I am," Jamie said as she surrendered.

THE NEW MAN

It started like it usually did, a new man Christi met at Alcoholics Anonymous, a night or two of drinking, then the pills hidden in the house. Jamie always found them though. Christi couldn't put anything past her. She had to get out. She called the old man with whom she had been hanging out. He was evil. She knew that. Already, he had violated her in sick ways, but he had a warm home and access to anything she wanted.

"You can't go out with that old man," Jamie argued. She had already banned her sister from taking her baby out alone, because she had used a private walk with him to meet this drug dealer. Jamie shuddered at the thought that their sweet little boy had been anywhere near this person. Now she was leaving her son to go out with him. "He's just some old drug-dealing pervert trying to get a young girl. I know he gave you pills."

"I can do whatever I want!" Christi yelled.

"Please, honey, don't do this. You are not well," Frances pleaded. It seemed she was always pleading with her daughter as she had with her father and her husband.

"You don't trust me! I am not going to use anything. I can't stay in this house and take care of a baby and never, ever go anywhere! I am not a prisoner!"

"You're not going," her mother said with firmness this time. She was so calm. Jamie wondered how in the world her mother could be so calm.

"I'm going." Christi grabbed her purse and left.

The baby began to cry, and Jamie and Frances tried to comfort him. It sometimes took the three of them—his grandfather, grandmother, and aunt—to calm him down. They would walk him for hours. Every little sound seemed to startle him into hysteria.

His mother did not come home that night or the next. Christi's family tried to focus on caring for her child. When she finally showed up days later, she was disheveled and in the same clothes. She had obviously been on a binge. They let her sleep it off and get something to eat, and then sat down to confront her.

"I'm not going to the hospital!" she shouted.

"If you don't get help, social services could take the baby," her sister warned.

"No one is going to take my baby!" Christi yelled.

Jamie felt sick hearing the same words from her sister's mouth that she had said before she had lost her girls.

"Everyone needs to stop telling me what to do!" Christi screamed again.

Their stepfather had been holding the baby in the chair by the sliding glass window, and the baby began to scream.

"Don't yell! You know how much loud noises bother him," Jamie said, angry now. She tried to calm the baby on his grandfather's lap, but he was trembling.

"I'm leaving." Christi turned to go out the door.

"You're not leaving." Jamie, who knew better, blocked the door.

Christi shouted profanities at her sister and turned to go out of the house. Her mother followed close behind. As the door to the porch swung open, Christi saw a chair and kicked it angrily. It flew across the porch, smashing into the glass door with her stepfather and baby behind it. The baby screamed, terrified, and Frances and Jamie ran to comfort him. His mother was gone.

It was not long before social services found out what was going on. Christi was forced to leave the home and her son behind. That night, Jamie held the tiny infant in her arms, and a tear ran down her cheek. She began sobbing quietly so as not to wake him. She had hardened her soul so much that no one had gotten in since this little boy's sisters, but now she was taking him in, taking him into the place she no longer let anyone go. She had no choice. Her sister had always said that someday, she would have a child for her, but in fact, this little boy wasn't hers. He needed her to love him with a mother's love, but as long as her sister was in the picture, she would never be his mom. She would be trapped again in this weird, nameless, frightening position. She could love him as if he had come from her body. She could raise and meet his every need for years, but at any time, her sister could get well and take him away. How could she put herself in this position again? It had nearly killed her the first time. The little boy in her arms opened his eyes and looked at her with a tired smile.

How can I not? she thought. *He needs me. Every child needs a parent to count on, and just loving him is such an amazing gift.*

THE ADDICTED ONE AND HER OTHER SIBLINGS

Christi's family had been separated long before her addiction had taken over her life. Paul lived on a farm alone in the country up north in Ohio. He had come down to try to fix the situation. Surely, his little sister wouldn't give him the trouble she gave their mother, who was far too tenderhearted and pacifying for him. Paul, however, found Christi a bit more to handle than he had thought. He caught her sneaking out one night and sent her to her room like a child, and then the cop in him told him to check the back window. The moment was almost comical as she climbed out only to turn and find him waiting for her. He was proud he had caught her, that he could control her better than they had. At least that was what he believed until the local police showed up at the door. Christi admitted she wanted to do crack and reported that he would not let her leave. She had called to have him arrested for kidnapping. The police said that Paul had no choice but to let her go or go to jail. Since she was not suicidal, they had to let her go. However, Paul, being the fighter, pulled the distributor wire off her car so she couldn't go anywhere. Later, he admitted to Frances and Jamie that he could not keep up with Christi. It took too much energy, and he didn't have the strength.

On another occasion, when Christi, crazed with drugs and hearing voices, was being admitted to the hospital, Paul was there. She fought the attendants as they tried to strap her down. Her brother, the one who was so strong and hardened, could not bear the humiliation they were putting her through and tenderly but firmly took hold of her arms and held her there so that she would not be hurt or hurt anyone. It was an act of love, and she would remember it as such.

Social services would no longer allow Frances to take Christi back in the house with the baby there. It was a blessing in a way, because Frances's health was deteriorating, and the baby was so fragile. Christi bounced around between halfway houses during this time. She would often call Tim late at night to cry, talk, and yell about her life. He dreaded those calls and, at times, would ignore them when they came in. He knew it would be an hour of painful conversation, usually with Christi blaming someone else for her problems. Tim would try to make suggestions, suggestions he knew would be ignored, but his sister always felt better after talking to him. They had been buddies as children, and despite their geographical distance, she felt close to him still. Christi felt like her brother understood her pain, and she never felt shame when the two of them talked. She had no clue how much Tim dreaded those calls. Despite loving her, he was tired of the repetitive nature of the calls and of the inevitable requests. One thing was completely predictable. Anytime Christi would start the conversation with "How are you doing?" she would be asking for money within the next ten minutes.

Money and drug addicts are a bad combination, and Tim struggled intensely with the choice of when to send Christi money and when to withhold it. As long as she was clean, he would pay for her housing and food needs. He was not dumb enough to send her cash (although she always tried to get it), but it was hard to tell.

The last time she called asking for money was a difficult conversation. Tim knew that Christi had been bingeing for weeks, and he just couldn't support her when she was using drugs. She was different this time, accepting of being denied, understanding that she had to do this herself. He wondered why she had accepted it so easily.

He didn't know the events that had taken place that week. Down on her knees, her mother was also down on her knees in a church two hundred miles away. Christi had finally made her choice between God and the devil, and she chose God. She had finally hit bottom and was ready to turn her life around. That week, she was staying at the Salvation Army shelter, and she seemed happier than she had been in years. She had some old friends there, and they had given her a certificate to get new clothes. She was so excited about shopping. Her mother was going to Chicago that weekend to visit Tim, and Christi didn't seem to mind. She told Frances not to worry. She was happy. She was now in a good place.

THE DOOR

Jamie had just finished bathing Christi's three-year-old. She had been relieved that her sister had not called to harass her the night before as she usually did when their parents left. It was getting late, and she had not heard from Christi yet, which seemed strange. Jamie rocked the little boy in her arms, trying to comfort him, to help his damaged nerves put themselves back in order. The last few weeks had been a struggle. She wanted to protect him from all the chaos. Then there was the prayer. Earlier that week, she had been praying about what to do, and God had given her the strangest message. The words rang in Jamie's spirit, not her ears. It was a message she was supposed to give her mother, but she didn't know how. The message was "Tell your mother that I still love our little girl."

A few days later, Christi called. She had been on her knees and had accepted God back into her life. Jamie had no idea what all of it meant, but she knew God had a plan. Yes, it had been a strange week.

As she sat there rocking the boy, reflecting on the prayer, there was a knock on the door. Jamie picked up the precious little boy and walked to the door. Her hand stopped as she reached for the door. She saw the familiar blue—the blue of a policeman's jacket. She felt her whole body quake, and she held the child tighter as she opened the door. She would never go to that door again without the memory of that day. Sometimes, God answers prayers in ways that we do not want or expect.

CHAPTER 14

ARE YOU AN ADDICTED ONE?

UNDERSTANDING THE ADDICTED ONE

Few people in life are judged more harshly than those who struggle with addictions. They are seen as weak at one end of the spectrum and evil at the other. We have found that many Addicted Ones can be the softest of the soft souls. Often, the pain of the world has become so great that they feel no choice but to become dependent on something that takes away that pain. In fact, Edgar Allan Poe once said, "I have absolutely no pleasure in the stimulants in which I sometimes so madly indulge. It has not been in the pursuit of pleasure that I have periled life and reputation and reason. It has been the desperate attempt to escape from torturing memories, from a sense of insupportable loneliness and a dread of some strange impending doom." We think that this is the experience of many who struggle with intense addictions; they are looking for escape or relief. Of course, the "cure" is short-lived and often creates a vicious cycle of temporary relief and then intense shame.

The never-ending cycle constantly reinforces itself and thus leads many addictions to continue to worsen until the person hits rock bottom or, in many cases, dies. Addictions destroy lives—not just the Addicted One's life but potentially the lives of others. As the addiction grows, the drive to obtain the substance of choice often becomes more important than health, friends, and family. While Addicted Ones could have any other archetype as part of their personality, they are sometimes described as the rebel, the misfit, or the wild one.

Of course, addictions can come in many forms. Here is a partial list of things to which we can become addicted:

- Alcohol
- Illegal drugs
- Prescription drugs
- Shopping or spending money
- Food
- Adrenaline
- Sex/pornography
- Gambling
- Hoarding
- Smoking
- Our job (workaholics)

There are two main components that differentiate a substance we simply enjoy or a habit we have from an actual addiction. The first is about our level of control. Can we control our participation in the substance or activity? While habits can be difficult to break, it is within our control to change them. Second, is the substance or activity harming us or others around us? Addictions cause great harm and usually continue to grow to a point where health, people, or relationships suffer.

Major Tendencies

Addicted Ones usually suffer from great shame and guilt concerning their addictions. Unfortunately, these negative emotions simply contribute to the pain that they are trying to distract themselves from and thus reinforce their addictions. Their tendencies can shift dramatically from defensiveness and denial to these feelings of shame and low self-esteem. As their emotions continue to spiral in a negative direction, their addictions increase. After being addicted for years, they can lose their identities and become people they don't want to be. They move from being gentle, soft souls to people who would sacrifice anyone and anything to get the next fix. They can go from soft, kind individuals to liars and cheats, completely abandoning the people they were meant to be.

The Positive Aspects

It seems difficult at first to find positive aspects in addiction. That said, many people with addictive personalities focus their addictions toward creating, building, and impacting lives for the positive. They can be incredibly focused and show dedication, hard work, and intensity that most can only imagine. On some level, Olympic athletes are addicted to exercise. On some level, individuals who create great companies and supply jobs to many people are addicted to success. While even these addictions taken too far can be damaging, if done at a healthy level, these and other addictions can serve the world and help others.

The Shadow Side

The shadow side of addiction is all too apparent: poor health, early death, deceived loved ones, lost relationships, theft—the list simply goes on and on and on. No child should be sacrificed for the love of a drug. No friendship should be lost because of stupid things said when you are drunk out of your mind. And no human being should have to live in shame, despising themselves when they sober up.

Strategies for Integrating Your Soft Soul While Honoring Your Addictive Tendencies

- We encourage you to seek help if drugs or alcohol (or any other addictions) have trapped you in a cycle of shame and destruction. Do it for yourself, and do it for those who love you. Explore the triggers that are catalysts for you turning to these habits. Find a replacement comfort such as meditation, prayer, talking to responsible friends, etc. If your problem has reached destructive levels, please reach out for professional help. Never, ever give up the battle.

- Remember that not all addictions are harmful. If you have an addictive personality, what addiction might be helpful to you? Examples include exercise or success. Or if it is not a full-blown addiction, could you integrate your substance into your life in a healthy way? For example, could a glass or two of wine be beneficial to you, and could you keep it to that level?

- Look at the people in your life who contribute in some way to your addiction. Are they helpful, loving, patient, and kind, and do they build you up? Or do they harm you, mislead you, and tear you down? Do you need to set appropriate boundaries to protect yourself from them, even if they are family members?

- Find a mentor who has walked your path, and ask for help. Make sure it is someone who understands your journey and has conquered their own demons. Also, remember to listen to the voice inside of you that encourages you and leads you to positive things in life.

- Do not judge yourself by your failures or the critique of others but rather by the love that your Creator has for you. Addicted Ones tend to live in shame of their addiction, which is often exacerbated by others. They then return to their drug of choice to deaden the pain. They base their self-value on their behavior or how others view them. God is the only being whose opinion about you is truly significant. You will fail others; you will fail yourself. God's grace for you is unfailing. You are beautiful to Him, you have a purpose for Him, and God does not waste any of His creations.

CHAPTER 15

BLESSED ARE THOSE WHO MOURN

A Funeral for a Soft Soul

CHRISTI'S HAIR

Frances reached to try to straighten her daughter's hair. It just didn't look right. Her youngest daughter had been so very meticulous about her hair since she was a teen, almost to obsession. Christi had a gift with hair. She spent hours in front of a mirror, curling and combing her auburn locks into lovely perfect waves on which people often commented. Her insistence on its perfection was an inside joke with the whole family.

There were no mirrors in that hollow room, and Christi, her baby, could no longer fix her own hair. Frances's hands trembled as she reached into her beloved daughter's casket and brushed her bangs from her still, shut eyes. She didn't want her grandchildren seeing their mother with her hair wrong. What an odd thing to think about. They were coming to see their mother's dead body the next day, and she was worried about her hair. Frances knew it would mean something deeper to them. Her breath left her for a moment, and she fought to take in another. How had her life come to this? Her worst fears had all come true.

Frances felt a rush of panic. She couldn't fix it. Her daughter's hair, now dull and lifeless, would not yield to her touch, just as her little child had not yielded to her mother's pleas to stay away from the people who would bring her out of her sobriety and take her on the path of death. Had drugs ended her life? They would not know for months. She had died in her sleep at the Salvation Army shelter. Only months later did they find out that her liver had just given out.

A SONG FOR CHRISTI

Paul sang a beautiful song at his sister's funeral; his strength was incredible as he managed to get through the entire song without falling apart. This was the gift of Paul. He had control and discipline over emotions.

He walked up on stage and started singing.

No more night. No more pain.

He could feel the emotion begin to well up, but he simply pushed it down.

No more tears. Never crying again.

His voice barely trembled as he fought to continue.

It's not a dream. God will make all things new that day.

Paul's voice carried throughout the church as he ended.

All praises to the great "I AM." We're gonna live in the light of the risen Lamb.

As he finished, Paul started to step down from the stage. His legs buckled, and his shoulders slumped while his body violently shook as tears came gushing from him. Paul sang the song to honor his sister, but afterward, there was only a little boy who missed his little sister.

A EULOGY FOR THE ADDICTED ONE

Tim choked back his tears as he stood before the crowd of relatives, friends, and addicts from the Salvation Army shelter to find some last words to honor his sister. He wondered as he spoke if her death was his fault. Was it because he wouldn't give her money that she was in that Salvation Army shelter? He had to remove his guilt and his doubt; his job was to bring peace and comfort to those present, and he so wanted to please his mother with his words. Here is what he said.

IN HONOR OF CHRISTI

In the Bible, in Luke, chapter 15, is a parable that I love. It is the parable Christ shared of the lost sheep. In the story, the shepherd is tending to his flock, and he notices that one of his sheep is missing. That sheep had wandered off and gotten lost. The shepherd has a choice at that point. Does he stay with the flock and just write off that single lost sheep, or does he drop what he is doing and go searching for that lost lamb? In Luke, chapter 15, the shepherd did not hesitate to go looking for the lost lamb. He dropped what he was doing and went out looking for the poor lost and frightened treasure. This is what Luke 15:6 has to say about the shepherd finding the lost sheep: "And when he comes home, he calls together his friends and neighbors, saying to them, 'Rejoice for me, for I have found my sheep which was lost.'"

Tim stopped, gathering his composure, and then continued.

Christi was God's lost sheep. She was His treasure who wandered off years ago. In the early hours of Saturday morning, January 25, in a warm, safe place, God sought out and reclaimed His lost treasure. He celebrates with her in heaven today. He loves His poor lost sheep, and He is holding Christi close to His heart. Today, we gather both to mourn our loss and to celebrate His gain that my sister, God's prodigal child, God's little lamb, is in His arms today.

As a child, Christi was all shy and sweetness. She was the baby of the family, and as with most families, we all doted on the baby. She was a cuddly little girl who loved to hug and be held. She couldn't be loved enough. As a girl, Christi came out of her shell. She was the life of the party. She definitely was the coolest of her siblings. As the main token nerd of this family, I know that this is definitely true. People loved her. Everyone around her was captivated by her smile and laughter. As a young mother, she was caring and loving. Now she was the one captivated by the beauty and innocence of her own children, first with her eldest daughter, then her second, and then finally with her son. She deeply, deeply loved her children.

We all know that in her adult years, Christi was troubled. We cannot and should not deny that reality. Her life was hard, and at times, it seemed like she wasn't the woman, sister, or mother that we knew. And yet, even in these last difficult years, those qualities that really made her Christi were still there, and we still adored them. When she was herself, Christi was hysterical. She was funnier than the rest of us and still could make us laugh. When she made mistakes, she would come back to apologize. She always felt terrible when she hurt people. In her imperfect human way, she still loved everyone in this room deeply.

Years ago, I made a terrible mistake that could have devastated those I love most due to selfishness and pride. In my shame, I called my family to tell them. While all of them were wonderful and forgiving, Christi did something even more for me...she knew. She knew what it was like to be weak. She knew what it was like to fail. She knew what it was like to deeply hurt those who you love most. She fully understood the pain that comes when we realize how human all of us truly are. She forgave me instantly for being human. I can do no less for her. Christi fought an illness and an addiction. And when I say fought, I mean fought. I've lost count of the number of programs that she went to. I've lost track of the number of meetings that she attended. I don't know the exact number of times that she tried. But I know this: she tried, she tried, she tried.

As tears welled up in his eyes, Tim continued.

When I think about what my baby sister would say if she were here, now that she is at peace and is fully herself again, this is what I think she would say. I believe that she would say, "I'm sorry for the pain that I have caused. Please forgive me, because your love is so important to me. Don't repeat my mistakes. Don't harbor the pain that I have caused in your heart. Do whatever you need to do to heal. Cry, yell, mourn, scream, pray, but heal. Heal in a way that I never could. Heal in a way that brings peace to your heart and love to your soul. Heal in a way that allows you to remember the good times and the times when you knew that I loved you with all of my heart."

I don't know for sure what Christi would say if she were here, but I do believe that she would want to say a few words to specific people. To all of the friends and family members who walked with her step by step through the last many years, most prominently Mom, our stepfather, and Jamie, she would say, "Thank you for supporting me so many times and in so many ways. From the thousands of phone calls, to holding me when I was in pain, to driving me, to confronting me when I was wrong, to forgiving me each and every time, to nurturing my children. Thank you. I don't know what I would have done without you."

To her children, I think she would say, "Never, never mistake my problems for a lack of love. I loved you and continue to love you with all of my heart and soul. All of my heart and soul."

To her friends in this room who have similar struggles, I think that she would say, "Never, never, never give up. Depend on God, and never give up."

Christi was always so close to our mother, so I think that she would have to say something specifically to her. To our mother, I believe that Christi would say, "I'm so sorry. No mother should have to mourn the death of her child. I'm so, so sorry. Thank you for everything that you tried, because I know you tried so hard. Thank you for the countless sacrifices. You don't need to sacrifice anymore. You don't need to sacrifice anymore."

But my baby sister is not here, and we will never know for sure what she would say, but I do believe that she would also say to everyone in this room, "I love you, and I thank you for loving me. Please love God, for He has finally gifted me with the peace I didn't have in life."

If I close my eyes, I can see Christi. I see her healthy and whole. I see her smiling. I see that wonderful twinkle in her eyes, and her eyes communicate that it's OK. She is OK. I see Christ next to her. He's holding her hand. His love fills her, and it is enough. It is finally enough. On her other side, I see her grandmother, Nanny. She is young and vibrant and is holding her other hand. Christi always loved Nanny. And behind her with his hands on her shoulders is her father, Ken. He is healthy and happy, and there is forgiveness and peace between them. Then surrounding her are others: friends, relatives, and angels. Her cousin is there and many others who we have lost before her.

But when I open my eyes, I realize that I don't really know

exactly what heaven is like. I don't really know what we look like when we go there. I don't really know how it all works. But this I know. This I know with all of my heart. I know that God loves us. And I know that He wants our love too. He doesn't just want us to know that He exists. He doesn't just want to be our higher power. He wants our complete and total devotion and love; nothing more, nothing less. He wants all of our love.

Last week, Christi was talking with our mother, and these are the words that she said. With deep sorrow in her voice, she sobbed, "When I think about what Jesus did for me on the cross, it breaks my heart in two. He took all my grief, all my sin, and all my sorrow. He died for me."

These were words that Christi spoke last week. These words give us peace, because while I don't know for sure what heaven looks like, I do know for sure that Nanny loved God. My father loved God. My cousin loved God. And my dear, sweet, beautiful sister, that lost little lamb, that adorable treasure...she... loved...God.

Please, please, please...love God.

As the service ended and mourning family members and friends left the church in silence, Frances and Jamie did what they always did. They cared for Christi's children.

Christi with her three children shortly before she died

A thing of beauty is a joy forever:

Its loveliness increases; it will never

Pass into nothingness; but still will keep

A bower quiet for us, and a sleep

Full of sweet dreams, and health, and quiet breathing.

—John Keats

PART THREE

HEALING THE SOFT SOUL IN PAIN

CHAPTER 16

MOURNING THE PAIN
OF THE WORLD

"Give sorrow words; the grief that does not speak knits up the o-er wrought heart and bids it break."

—William Shakespeare, *Macbeth*

THE STRUGGLE OF THE SOFT SOUL

W<small>E HAVE SHARED WITH YOU THE TRUE STORY OF A FAMILY OF SOFT SOULS,</small> and we will come back to their story later in this book, but this family is not unique. They are but one of thousands of families who face the struggle of the soft soul daily. You may see them in your own family: the Idealist who holds on too long when things aren't working, the Charmer who ends up becoming a manipulator and hurting others, the Fighter who finds battles everywhere he goes, the Pleaser who feels responsible for giving others peace and takes too much on his shoulders, the Invisible One who gives up on fully expressing herself and being seen by the world, or an Addicted One who goes to substances to escape. These types exist in so many families. Maybe you see yourself in their stories. Your authors, a psychologist and a former teacher, have seen these six different reactions to being a soft soul with many people.

The soft soul's dilemma in this world is the ultimate paradox. If you stay a soft soul, the world tends to crush you. If you harden your soul, you cut yourself off from the beautiful, genuine part of you that makes you the person your Creator intended you to be. Stay soft, and you experience constant disappointments and hurts. Harden yourself, and you lose that special piece of your humanity.

A UNIVERSAL TRUTH FOR ALL SOFT SOULS

There is one thing that all soft souls need to do to move beyond their past—to truly heal, we must experience our grief but not get lost in it. There are many types of grief. We grieve for the dreams we have lost, for the loves that have slipped through our hands, for things we have left undone or unsaid until it was too late, and for the ones we had hoped we could change but never did. Soft souls mourn deeply. This is not simply the process of letting ourselves feel loss but rather a guttural, primal, heart-aching, painful mourning that comes from acceptance. In this painful acceptance, we fully realize that we are not in control of everything that happens to us and that we are ultimately, frailly, imperfectly human. For some, this is a horrid thing to have to admit and feel.

So we must mourn, but we cannot just mourn the loss of others or things we desired for our lives. There is a person we must mourn who we often do not even acknowledge we have lost. In many ways, the loss of that person is the greatest loss to our lives. That person is the soft soul that our Creator formed us to be, the soul He created to rejoice, to love without ceasing, to imitate His soul. Few of us can maintain that soul living in a harsh, hard world. We must mourn the loss of the person we were made to be in order to develop the person we were made to become, a still soft but stronger soul. This experience often comes in later life when we realize the damage that has been done to our soul from all the hardships we have faced. It is the stage where we mourn the loss of the person we once were, whose soul was soft enough to take a risk on love, vulnerable enough to sincerely care for others, and tender enough to feel the presence of God in a powerful, fully trusting way. Almost all of us get to this stage at one point or another. It may come on suddenly when we hear ourselves say something harsh and unredeeming, something we would never have dreamed we would say. Sometimes, it is a gradual process, when we find ourselves caring less and less about our friends and neighbors and focusing more on our own success and survival. The revelation can come in many ways, and the revelation tells us that we were meant to be something different, something better.

THE TWO EXTREMES:
REPRESSING OR RECYCLING OUR PAIN

There are two *extreme* ways of dealing with our deep mourning, and both can be destructive to the soft soul. Some people tend to repress their pain, which often turns that pain into a ticking time bomb that will explode later in life. Others get into the habit of recycling and re-experiencing their pain repeatedly, which turns their pain into constant suffering and destroys any chance of living a meaningful life in the present. Mourning allows us to release pain that can become toxic to our souls if contained. Sometimes, we are so hurt by the world that we repress our painful experiences and build up emotional walls that lead to deadened lives. We are in need of a cleansing of our souls so we can live again. Soul cleansing must take place before we can return to our genuine soft state. This cleansing starts with mourning deeply.

This is not simply having a good cry or locking ourselves away from the world for a few days. This is an opening up of our souls and letting ourselves experience the pain that we shoved away because we thought we would not survive if we really allowed ourselves to feel all of the pain. It is taking all of that heartrending grief and holding it into the light for our Creator to see and to heal. It seems a reasonable thing to do, and yet, for some reason, it seems to be our last action. Many of us are terrified of our hurtful experiences and doubt whether our souls can survive the emotions connected with them. We try to nurse our wounds with work, with medication, by throwing ourselves into caring for others, or by obsessively serving some cause. Worse, we allow ourselves to fall into acts we despise, such as drowning our sorrows in drugs, sex, and alcohol. We do anything (or, more precisely, everything) we can in order to avoid feeling the pain. We need to experience our pain in order to release our pain. The Bible is full of psalms that demonstrate this. Take, for example, David's crying out in Psalm 38:4–10 from the Bible (New International Version):

My guilt has overwhelmed me like a burden too heavy to bear. My wounds fester and are loathsome because of my sinful folly. I am bowed down and brought very low; all day long I go about mourning. My back is filled with searing pain; there is no health in my body. I am feeble and utterly crushed; I groan in anguish of heart. All my longings lie open before you, Lord; my sighing is not hidden from you. My heart pounds, my strength fails me; even the light has gone from my eyes.

The writer is obviously expressing many emotions, including the pain of his soft soul. We believe these psalms are in the Bible to let us know that it is acceptable to express our grief, especially to God.

Repressing pain can lead to losing joy for life. For many, the cost of escaping sorrow also means escaping joy. If you deaden negative emotions, it might mean that your positive emotions pay the same cost. So you live in a manner that avoids negative emotional experiences, but you create a life with no highs either. For some, this stability is worth the cost. For others, they are living knowing that they are missing out on some wonderful, tender, joyous parts of life.

Repressing emotions is one extreme and unproductive way that soft souls deal poorly with their tendency to feel things deeply. The other extreme is to recycle the pain. Recycling the pain in our lives leads us to live in a constant state of victimhood. We remember and feel the hurts of yesterday as if they are happening today. Every unkind word or act of aggression against our soft souls is remembered and experienced over and over. We go from someone who was hurt badly to someone who *lives* in suffering. Memories carry the same intensity as current events and can taint our experience of our lives *now*, in the moment. Individuals who have been hurt and have fallen into the trap of recycling pain see aggressors and danger in every corner. They live like war veterans in a state of post-traumatic stress. As a soldier may experience the sounds of a lawn sprinkler bringing back the visions of enemy helicopters, so a victim of abuse, betrayal, or loss may be triggered by sounds, sights, smells, or any other reminder of the past. Recycling is an understandable reaction, especially for those who have experienced multiple painful events, but recycling the past pain of your life guarantees that your present life will never be what it could be.

We must also clarify that living in the past sorrow and venting the pain of the past are not the same thing. At times, venting may look like recycling, but there are major differences. Venting is done with the intent to release the pain, is shorter in duration, and results in peace. Recycling merely causes the person to reexperience the pain, can last a lifetime, and creates immeasurable and unending suffering.

So what is your strategy for handling your pain? Are you a soft soul who does not want to release your pain because you fear that you will drop your guard and get hurt again? Do you remain in a constant state of vigilance? Or do you subconsciously keep your pain alive in order to punish your aggressor by not letting him off the hook? Of course, the main person you are hurting is yourself. A philosopher once said that we can be either a student or a victim of life. When we recycle, we develop the identity of a victim.

Recycling pain can be just as devastating to a life as repressing pain. Automobiles have a rearview mirror for a reason. We look in the rearview mirror to see what is behind us. Glancing into your rearview mirror is necessary before you make a lane change and could even save your life if you have someone speeding up from behind you. However, a driver has to just glance in the rearview mirror and not get stuck staring at it. A driver who looks into the rearview mirror will miss what is going on to the front and sides and will likely crash the car. Drivers must focus on where they are going and simply check now and then for what is behind them. It is just like that in life. We need to acknowledge, feel, understand, and stay aware of our past. We must also acknowledge that it is behind us, focus on what is going on in our life today, and also actively create the life we want in our future. Otherwise, we crash our life and blame all of the other bad drivers on the road.

By resolving to neither repress nor recycle, by releasing emotional ghosts that haunt you, and by renewing your focus and energy, you can hone the beautiful, tender power of your soft soul to live with deep joy. A life with tears is not a life lacking joy. In truth, to fully experience life, you must have both. A life led by the heart is a life worth living.

The pain of grief is just as much a part of life as the joy of love; it is, perhaps, the price we pay for love, the cost of commitment. To ignore this fact, or to pretend that it is not so, is to put on emotional blinkers which leave us unprepared for the losses that will inevitably occur in our own lives and unprepared to help others cope with losses in theirs.

—*Dr. Colin Murray Parkes*

CHAPTER 17

RESTORING THE PURITY OF YOUR HEART

If you want to forget something or someone, never hate it, or never hate him/her. Everything and everyone that you hate is engraved upon your heart; if you want to let go of something, if you want to forget, you cannot hate.

—C. JoyBell C.

THE PLIGHT OF THE SOFT SOUL IS FILLED WITH CHALLENGES AND PAIN, AND there is no magic wand that will remove all of that pain. The world is often harsh. The world can be quite painful, and the only sane thing to do in the face of man's inhumanity to man, nature's destructive ways, and various injustices is to feel the pain and fall back into the arms of God. Yet, for every unkind behavior, we can find an act of kindness. For every destructive act of nature, we can find another example of beauty. And for every injustice, we can hope for the ultimate justice in eternity. Soft souls must remember this, or they will get lost in the pain and lose themselves to the world.

While the answer to surviving tough times may rest in releasing but not recycling the past, the answer to thriving lies not in changing or hiding your soft soul but rather in embracing it to the fullest. The key to thriving is to love. However, loving deeply is trickier than one might think, and we need to talk about what to love. In this chapter, we will address five things you must completely love in order to thrive as a soft soul:

- Love yourself
- Love your life
- Love your future
- Love your neighbor
- Love your God

LOVE YOURSELF

While it may sound cliché, loving yourself is the first step for healing your soft soul. Often, people who realize that they are soft souls hate the way they are built. They wish they felt less. They wish they could just ease through life the way some other people seem to do. So step one for soft souls is to fully love who they are and how they have been created. What do you do when you love someone? First, you listen to them—no one feels loved if they don't feel heard. Soft souls must listen to their inner dialogue. What do they want? What do they not want? They must trust their judgment and their instincts—all aspects of themselves. Before acting, they must listen.

Next, soft souls need to embrace their flaws (or at least perceived flaws). These are the things that make you, well, you! Only when you learn to show yourself mercy and care will you be able to work on those flaws. Shame and guilt interfere with growth, while conviction leads to personal evolution. Show yourself patience as you walk through this journey and continue to grow and change. Give yourself forgiveness and grace rather than judgment and punishment.

Along with loving who you are, you must also learn to love your body, whatever it is—fat, skinny, short, tall, smooth, wrinkly. When we love our bodies, we take care of them. When we hate them, we subject them to substance abuse (including food and alcohol), yo-yo diets, or just general self-destructive behavior. Learn to treat your body with respect and care. If you don't like something about your body that you are able to change, gently and caringly work to change it, not through shame, but rather through love. Loving your body as it is will often be the key to changing the things about your body that you don't find ideal.

The next thing you need to love about yourself is your heart. Yes, some of you are highly sensitive. Yes, some of you are dramatic at times. Yes, some of you are moody and can brood on your emotions, but most of you are that way simply because you feel deeply. To bury that is to bury the essence that makes you lovely and loving and a gift to others around you. Certainly, you can learn different methods to make sure your emotions are not harmful to yourself or others, but we don't want you to hide that part of you that can impact your life and everyone around you for the positive. Love your heart, and channel it toward giving back to the world, even when the world has been tough on you. The best way to do that is to take the next step in loving yourself—you must guard your mind.

Because soft souls feel deeply, they can be caught in some of the illusions of this world. These illusions are common perceptions that are simply not true and cause a significant amount of false pain for the soft soul. Cognitive behavioral psychologists have uncovered a number of irrational beliefs that create this phantom pain. There are many, but some of the most common for soft souls include:

- Everyone must love me in order for me to be worthwhile.
- Rejection is a terrible thing and means there is something wrong with me.

- I must be perfect.
- It is terrible if I'm not appreciated for something I did for someone.
- It is always my fault.
- I am cursed.

These thoughts seem so true for many soft souls but are, in fact, simply junk from their past. Do you doubt this? Then imagine this—imagine someone you love deeply, and imagine them sitting across the room from you. Now say to them the following:

- You are worthless if everyone doesn't love you.
- Every time you get rejected, it is because there is something wrong with you.
- You must be perfect at all times.
- It is a horrible tragedy if someone doesn't appreciate something you did.
- It is always your fault.
- You are cursed.

Who would ever say these lies to someone they loved? No one! So love yourself enough to guard your mind from these and other lies. If someone rejects or doesn't appreciate you, simply let it hurt, and do not allow it to create an illusion of your inadequacy!

The last way to love yourself that we want to address in this section is to give yourself a voice. Just because you are a soft soul does not mean that you can't allow yourself to speak the truth. While psychologists focus on teaching assertiveness skills (which are not bad in and of themselves), we would rather encourage you to simply speak the truth as you know it and speak it with respect for yourself as well as for others. Sometimes, soft souls only speak the truth once it has built up, and then, it is often expressed with anger (which then leads to embarrassment or shame). By allowing yourself an honest and loving voice, you will keep from building bitterness while impacting others around you for the positive.

Suggested Tactics

In order to listen to yourself, you could start keeping an emotional journal of what is going on both outside of you (the events around you) and inside of you (your inner dialogue and feelings).

For embracing your flaws or guarding your mind, you could use your journal to gain insight into self-criticism and replace those thoughts with self-statements around accepting and embracing your flaws.

For loving your body, you can slowly ease into an exercise program and listen to your body before you eat (not your taste buds). Does your body really want that food or drink? Listen and follow the instructions. Choose to love your body enough to take care of it! By the way, both of your authors do all of the above imperfectly (even though we write about it), so please accept that you will do this in a flawed way. You do not need to be perfect. Love all of those imperfections!

LOVE YOUR LIFE

Because they feel pain so deeply, soft souls often get lost in the difficulties of life. They feel like victims to the harder souls and can, at times, forget about all of their blessings. One key to working through your hurt is to fully embrace it. By embracing your pain, you will experience the pain, but you will not put self-imposed suffering on top of your pain. It is like going to the dentist. Most people tense up when they hear the drill. They fight the drill (or whatever tool the dentist is using), and this causes them to feel both the pain of the drill and the suffering that comes with resisting the drill. By choosing to embrace the drill (i.e., invite it into your mouth), you will only experience the pain of the drill and nothing else.

When we embrace our losses, we feel the mourning deeply, but we do *not* have to suffer as we feel it. You can't help it if you were abused, bullied, hurt, or betrayed. These things should hurt, and they do. You must face them, feel them, and embrace them as part of your journey. This means that you have to love your past. Find purpose in your challenges and hurts. Find strength and hope in the fact that you have endured them and made it! By embracing that your past has made you who you are, you only feel the pain of the original sins against you, and you get rid of the self-imposed pain. "I can't believe this happened to me!" creates both the original pain and the self-inflicted damage. "This happened to me, and I embrace that it is real, but it does not determine who I am and what I will do!" allows you to mourn the original pain and then celebrate your current victory.

Along with loving your past, you must also love your present. Every day that we wake up, we have a choice of what to focus on—the good or the bad. What is great about your life today? Do you have shelter and food? Sometimes, we can become so entitled that we forget that much of the world struggles daily for simple things to survive. We can make every moment in our life perfect by doing two things—owning it and finding purpose in it. John Chancellor wrote on teachthe-soul.com about a bit of research done with would-be neurosurgeons. In the study, they found that two questions could determine who was successful and who would eventually fail out of the program. The two questions were:

- Do you ever make mistakes?
- If so, what is the worst mistake you have ever made?

They found that anyone who said they rarely or never made mistakes failed out of the program. These were people who refused to look at themselves honestly. For the second question, they found that anyone who externalized the mistake (i.e., it was someone else's fault) also failed out of the program. Only people who took 100 percent ownership for their decisions succeeded in accomplishing the very difficult task of becoming a neurosurgeon.

When we own our lives, we empower ourselves. To focus on how others have victimized you (beyond healthy mourning) creates the identity of a victim. And what happens to victims? They get victimized! You are not a victim! Someone may have hurt you in the past, but embrace that you own your life. You can create what you want. You can choose to be happy. You can choose to embrace your past and love your present. No one can take that away from you unless you allow it.

Another key is to find purpose in every challenge. If we allow it, we can learn from every experience in life. When we find purpose in pain, we grow and mature. We become stronger by finding the purpose. We have more peace when we can make something positive out of something horrible. The author Viktor Frankl writes about this in *Man's Search for Meaning* as he recounts the horrors he experienced in a Nazi concentration camp during World War II. He notes that the people who hoarded their last piece of food often ended up dying, while those who gave away their last piece of food survived. They refused to let their circumstances dictate their identity. They found purpose in the struggles as they continued to help others despite the devastation that they experienced. If they could do that in concentration camps, then what excuse do we have to get lost in the pain? You can make every moment perfect by finding purpose in it.

Suggested Tactics

One great tactic for loving your life is to keep a gratitude journal. Keep track of everything for which you are grateful. These could be simple things, like beautiful weather, or bigger things, like a wonderful experience that you had while traveling. Also, any time you get a compliment, a nice email, or a card, or you have some success at something, put it in your gratitude journal. Then, when a tough day comes along, open up your journal and read all of these gems. It will remind you that the bad times are temporary. Living with gratitude is the antidote to living with bitterness. Philippians 4:8 in the Bible (New International Version) says it best:

Finally, brothers, whatever is true, whatever is noble, whatever is right, whatever is pure, whatever is lovely, whatever is admirable—if anything is excellent or praiseworthy—think about such things.

Another way to enjoy each moment is to simply stop and breathe. In all of the rush of our days, we sometimes forget to take a breath! Breathe in through your nose and out through your mouth. Breathe in life and happiness, and breathe out anything that you don't want living inside of you.

Finally, we find that filling your life with music, movies, and poetry that move you is a wonderful way to make each day meaningful and positive. And, of course, if anything bad happens to you, write it down, express your feelings, and then write down one to three potential purposes behind your trial. Write down one way to respond to the difficulty that has meaning and value, and then go execute!

LOVE YOUR FUTURE

Nothing in our past has to dictate our future. You can take two people from similar backgrounds, and one may become a criminal while another becomes a leader. We make choices every day that determine where we will be tomorrow. Your past does not dictate your future unless you allow it. In California, some wines are made out of mountain fruit. These grapes usually have to fight for their survival. Gravity and weather work against them, and they cling to life, fighting to get through the challenges in a way that grapes on flat land never have to fight. Not all grapes survive these conditions, but the grapes that weather the storm are intense, bold, and full of flavor. The fight for survival turns them into something spectacular. They are called stressed grapes, and there is a famous saying in Napa Valley, California: "Stressed grapes make the best wine." What wine could be created from the challenges that you have been through? Who can you help? What message do you have for the world? What would give you purpose and mission for the future? Love your future, and create it daily!

Suggested Tactics

Many people have benefited from creating visual depictions of what they want for their future. This could be done on a poster or in any form. The idea is to create a captivating vision of what you want for your work, life, relationships, family, living situation, or whatever applies. These depictions are highly effective, because the visual elements (versus the written word) hit the emotional parts of your brain. This can motivate and focus you to create this vision for your life.

Another tactic is to conduct a capabilities analysis and use it to help create what you want for your life. Simply answer the following questions (in writing):

1. What are your five greatest accomplishments in life so far? They can be from any stage of life but should be due to something you did versus something you simply accomplished due to luck.

2. What characteristics, abilities, talents, and personal tendencies contributed to your success in each of the five accomplishments?

3.   What is the biggest obstacle you defeated in your past?

4.   How did you do it?

5.   What is one thing you want to create for your future? This could be a habit to create or break or simply an accomplishment.

6.   How could you utilize the abilities and talents you wrote about earlier to create this positive outcome for your future?

7.   To whom could you be accountable to accomplish this?

We include that last question because having an accountability partner is one of the best ways to change something in your life. This should be someone positive who will not shame you but will encourage you to meet your goals and help you hold your feet to the fire!

LOVE YOUR NEIGHBOR

While loving the way you were designed, loving your life, and loving your future are crucial to your happiness, they are also just part of the solution for thriving as a soft soul. Those loves are just about you, and soft souls are built to love others. What would life be like if you made love your number one goal? Someone hurts you—love them. Someone is a stranger—love them. Someone is hurting themselves—love them. It is hard to go wrong when you love others. In this busy, busy world where we are captivated by technology and often separated from community, it is easy to get so distracted that we miss chances to love. A friend once told us, "There is always time for love." She is absolutely right. Moreover, we would add that there is always time for love if we prioritize it.

Now, first off, let's be careful not to confuse loving others with submitting yourself to someone who hurts you. If someone has a constant pattern of humiliating you emotionally or physically, we are absolutely not encouraging you to accept that in your life. If you love yourself, you can't live in constant fear for your safety. Therefore, we would encourage anyone in that situation to get help. Love yourself enough to reach out for assistance—you just don't have to hate the victimizer while you protect yourself.

But for those who are not in these extreme situations, you must always remember that people make mistakes. All of us have hurt someone at some time in our lives. Love others, and give them grace through their mistakes. Forgive others for the hurts they have done to you, because you will also need forgiveness at some point. Some of you may be thinking, "They don't deserve forgiveness!" Well, that is the tricky thing about forgiveness. You can only give forgiveness when they don't deserve it! If they do deserve it, then you are being unfair to them. You are the one who is doing wrong! We are only in the position to forgive someone who doesn't deserve it when we are justified in holding the hurt they have done to us over their heads. Do you want to do something good for your soft soul? Then go forgive someone who does not deserve your forgiveness.

On the other hand, if you are the soft soul who has built up walls or who has hurt someone else, you may need to be the person who asks for forgiveness. Love your neighbors enough to humbly go to them and ask them to forgive you. But do not try to force the issue. You cannot control whether or not they give you grace, and it is not your right to push someone to forgive you. Make amends the best you can, and leave the forgiveness in their hands.

That leads us to a very critical concept that all soft souls must understand— embracing your giftedness as a method to love others better and more fully. Think for a second on this question: what types of people irritate you the most? Is it "stupid" people? Rude people? Lazy people? Insensitive people? If not one of these four, what is it for you? What kinds of people bother you the most? Take a moment to think about that.

Now consider the opposite of that characteristic. For example, the opposite of stupid would be smart, rude would be polite, lazy would be people with a strong work ethic, and insensitive would, of course, be sensitive. What is the opposite of the characteristic that irritates you so much?

Here is the deal. Think about that opposite characteristic. Does that describe you? Are you "normal" when it comes to that characteristic? Are most people like you, or are you different from most? For the majority of you reading this book, you are probably gifted with the opposite characteristic of the people who irritate you. If stupid people irritate you, you are likely highly intelligent, or if rude people irritate you, you are likely a very polite soul. We tend to judge people most harshly in our area of giftedness. We mentally act as if they are outside the norm and something is wrong with them when, in reality, *you* are the one outside the norm! You are the one who is different. You have a gift! We must never forget this. If you forget you are gifted, you will judge and be hurt by people who do not possess that same gift. (They likely have other gifts.) When we realize that we have been blessed with that characteristic more than others, it creates patience instead of impatience, forgiveness rather than judgment, and a desire to mentor more than a desire to hurt. Embrace your gifts, and you will be more loving toward others.

Suggested Tactics

Make a giftedness list. Name one to three areas in which you are unusually gifted. Keep this list handy to help you have more patience and less frustration with your neighbors who don't have these gifts.

If you are having trouble letting go of something that someone did that hurt you in the past, write a venting letter. Write it to the person, but do *not* give it to them. Write it, read it aloud, and then do something symbolic to show that you are letting the hurt go. Do this as many times as needed. If you are blocked by the thought *But this lets them off the hook and says it was OK,* try to remember that they are not on a hook. The only hook is the one piercing you inside.

Then, make a list of people you may have hurt. Find a way to make amends with them through a letter or conversation. Take 100 percent responsibility for your own actions (even if the other person played a part in the problem). Request forgiveness, but remember that it is their right to keep their own hooks inside of them too.

Finally, we encourage you to surround yourself with positive people in your life. Even the most loving person on this planet struggles to stay positive and loving when they are surrounded by negative, unhappy people. We are not saying to completely cut off people who are stuck. We are just suggesting that if you are going to give energy to people, you also need to make sure your tank is full.

LOVE YOUR GOD

The last section in this chapter is perhaps the hardest to put in a book, because it is personal and can be controversial (and misunderstood). We want to first start by telling you that God is a mystery to us. We know what we believe today, but much of what we believe today is different from what we believed when we were younger. We make no claim to understanding God more than you do. But we simply cannot write this book without sharing our understanding and love for the Creator. What does it mean to truly love God? For us, this means doing our best to live a life that pleases Him. In Galatians 5:22–23, in the New International Version of the Bible, there is a verse that gives us some guidelines to know if we are letting God's spirit guide us:

But the fruit of the Spirit is love, joy, peace, forbearance, kindness, goodness, faithfulness, gentleness and self-control. Against such things there is no law.

We do these very imperfectly, but we continue to try, and we continue to be thankful to God for His grace and mercy, which we so desperately need. We also personally believe in Jesus as the Son of God and follow His example and His teachings (sometimes better than other times). Grace and forgiveness are beautiful things to us, and we love our God for giving those to us freely.

We also love God by worshipping Him. Through gathering with other believers and studying the Bible or through singing songs of worship, we want to show respect for the One who created all of this. Any being capable of creating the miracles that we find in everyday life deserves our praise and adoration. One of the authors' favorite forms of worship is to see God in nature and praise Him for the beautiful world He created.

We also love God by leaning into His arms when we are hurting, scared, or in need of comfort. A pastor once said, "You can only lean one way." How true is that statement! When we go through difficult times, we can either lean on our own understanding and capabilities or lean into the Creator, asking for guidance, strength, and comfort. This is also an act of respect, as we recognize that we are not in control, are not meant to save others, and yet are not alone.

This is how we love God. How do you? Because our beliefs are strong, we are sometimes misunderstood by people who believe differently than we do. At times, people have the misperception that we are judging them simply from the fact that we base our beliefs on the Bible. Conversely, because we are very tolerant of different perspectives, we are sometimes misunderstood by other Christians who misperceive our stance as saying that any religion is truth. We do not believe that all religions are the same. We also do not see it as our job to force our beliefs on anyone else. People have been tortured and killed for believing differently than the people in power. How this must sadden God! Our job, in our opinion, is to pursue and pray for truth, share what we believe unashamedly, and then encourage others to do the same. If you have a willing heart and sincerely ask for truth, we trust that God will reveal it to you in His time. One of your authors prays this prayer almost every week. We never want to be so arrogant as to think that we completely understand someone as big and powerful as the Lord of all creation. So pray for truth, and love your God.

Suggested Tactics

There are no magical tactics for loving God, so we simply encourage you to go out to a place in nature and pray, worship, read the Bible, and listen.

It is time to return to love. Love yourself, love your life, love your future, love your neighbor, and love God.

Darkness cannot drive out darkness: only light can do that. Hate cannot drive out hate: only love can do that.

—Martin Luther King Jr.

CHAPTER 18

PROTECTING AND RECHARGING YOUR SOFT SOUL

The best and most beautiful things in the world cannot be seen or even touched. They must be felt with the heart.

—Helen Keller

WHEN YOUR SOFT SOUL HAS EXPERIENCED INTENSE HARSHNESS, YOU CAN become disheartened, discouraged, or even depressed. Once you accept that you are a soft soul, it is important to commit to protecting yourself from unnecessary harm and taking the time to destress, relax, and recharge. Unlike other chapters that are mostly narrative with some tactics, this chapter has some narrative but primarily focuses on tactics you can use to protect and recharge. These are adapted from one of your authors' other books called *Tough Times Tactics*.

OVERCOMING FEAR

Living in fear will deplete your energy, drain your ambition, and just make you miserable. When human beings experience fear, they tend to have a fight-or-flight reaction; they go on the offensive or the defensive. A certain level of fear is not necessarily bad for you. Productive fear or worry can:

- Alert us to real dangers and lead us to solutions or to escaping the danger.
- Be realistic in its assessment of the threat.
- Turn our attention to things we can control and lead us to making a positive impact on these things.
- Help us know when to back off something and when to move ahead.
- Build our self-concept as a capable person who can navigate life.
- Protect us from harm.

Unproductive fear, on the other hand, can:

- Fail to lead us to any clear course of action.
- Waste our time with focusing on unlikely events.
- Catastrophize the future.
- Erode our confidence, sleep, and energy.
- Overestimate the true threat.
- Hurt our relationships, performance, or self-concept.

If you have experienced harm in the past, it can be difficult to live a life free of unproductive fear and worry. The problem is that our body often cannot tell the difference between an imagined consequence and something we really experienced. So when you imagine all of the terrible what-ifs for the future, your body might feel like you actually went through the horrific experience. This is draining on your soul.

For years when we were kids, we ran haunted houses during Halloween. We would put on the full production with dry ice, fog machines, dummies, chainsaws, scary music, and, of course, pop outs! However, it wasn't until we discovered one missing factor that our haunted houses went from *somewhat* scary to *really* scary. What was the missing factor? We needed to have times where *nothing* happened as people walked through the haunted house. When nothing was happening, people would be thinking, *What's going to happen? When is it going to happen? What is around the corner?* and other thoughts as they anticipated the pop outs. Then when we would finally pop out, they would jump to the roof! When we discovered that people have more of an ability to scare themselves than we had to scare them, we became true masters of running a haunted house.

Some people walk through life as if they were walking through a haunted house, constantly imagining all of the bad things that can happen. On a frequent basis, they scare themselves. The good news is, if we have the ability to cause such fear, then we also have the ability to decrease the fear. Let's examine a couple of tactics for decreasing fear.

Tactic #1: Take the "What-If" All the Way

What if I lose my job? What if I get sick? What if this relationship doesn't work out? We can drive ourselves crazy thinking about all of the what-ifs in life. If you can keep yourself from going there, that is great, but many people have a hard time stopping that process. We encourage these individuals to take the what-if all the way. *What if I lose my job?* OK, what if you lose your job? What would you do? How would you cope? How would you go about the job search? Who would you turn to for help? With this technique, you keep asking and answering those questions until you have a plan. By taking it all of the way and answering your own questions, you have moved the situation from ambiguity to strategy. This increases your confidence and decreases your fear.

Tactic #2: Control What You Say to Yourself

Rational-emotive behavior therapy is a form of therapy pioneered by Albert Ellis that addresses and helps replace self-defeating thoughts. Research has shown that changing these beliefs can lead to greater success, emotional stability, and happiness. The method below is based on this form of therapy and focuses on harmful things we can say to ourselves in the workplace. You can use this tactic for dealing with any irrational emotion, but we will focus on using it to deal with fear.

With practice, you can eliminate thoughts that cause you unproductive fear and replace them with a mind-set and attitude that will take you from paralyzing fear to confidence and action. The method below helps you do this in a structured manner that quickly helps you master your thoughts. There are multiple steps to the process:

1. Record the event or catalyst that is causing you to feel afraid.

2. Dig deep into your thought process to determine what you are saying to yourself that is causing you to feel that level of fear. Keep digging until you have come to the thought that causes the most fear. Make sure it is a statement rather than a question. Behind every question we ask ourselves is an answer that causes either a positive or negative reaction. For example, if you are asking yourself, "Can I handle this?" and your subconscious answer is yes, you feel great; if your answer is no, you feel badly. So discover the thought and write it down.

3.   Put the thought through two tests: is it 100 percent true, and does it help you to think this way? Obviously, if the thought is draining you or leading to unproductive fear, it is not helping you!

4.   If it passes both of these tests, keep it. If it fails *either* of these tests, replace it with a new thought that leads to eliminating any unproductive fear and/or leads to positive action.

5.   Practice the new thought constantly until your old thought is eliminated or highly minimized.

Let's go through an example. I (Tim) was doing a workshop for a company that had just merged with another company. As I was meeting one of the employees from the acquired company, I introduced myself as a coach who had been working for the other company for a number of years. After a short discussion, I left to go to the restroom. When I returned, the employee had his back to me, and I heard him say, "I hear that they are dumping the coach." Now, this was my number one client. My immediate reaction was fear, and it was intense. I knew immediately that I had to get this fear under control, because I was about to go onstage and lead the workshop. So, applying our method, this is what I did:

1.   The catalyst for my fear: I just overheard someone saying that they are dumping the coach.

2.   Self-talk: I am going to lose my number one client!

3.   Two tests: I could not prove that I was going to lose my client; I could only prove that I heard what this employee said. It was also not helpful for me to keep saying to myself, "I'm going to lose my number one client!" as I was going onstage to talk. It failed both tests.

4. New thought: I decided that my new thought would focus around gratitude, so I started saying to myself, "I am so grateful I heard that, because now I can focus on bringing my best to this presentation and convince them that they want to keep me."

5. Practice: I said it to myself as much as I could onstage.

By changing my self-talk, I managed to do a good job onstage. Later, I did go to that employee and mentioned what I heard him say. His response was, "Yes, the city's team has stunk for years, and it's about time they replaced him." Ironically, he wasn't even talking about me!

How often do we do this to ourselves? We get all worked up and full of fear over nothing. Again, productive fear is good, but let's eliminate the unproductive fear in our lives. Winston Churchill said, "When I look back on all these worries, I remember the story of the old man who said on his deathbed that he had had a lot of trouble in his life, most of which never happened." Get out of the haunted house, focus on what is real, not imagined, and tackle the real fears with courage and discernment.

REDUCING STRESS

Eliminating unproductive fear is a way to reduce stress that you are creating, but what about reducing stress that you are not creating? Fortunately, there are many methods for reducing stress, and which ones you use depend on your personality, your time, your income, and what truly works for you. Here is a list of stress-reducing tactics that our clients have shared with us over the years.

Exercise

Physical exercise changes your body chemistry, helps you create more energy, and makes you feel good about yourself. Also, if you add a mental component of imagining that you are releasing tension, anger, fear, stress, or whatever you need to release while you are working out, it works even better.

Venting

If you are an emotional person to your core, sometimes, you just need to release that emotion in a productive way that doesn't hurt anyone. This can be done verbally or in writing. It works best if you allow yourself to be really primal. Don't hold back (except if it would hurt you physically). We talked earlier in this book about how you can write a letter to the person with whom you are angry and then tear it up afterward to show that you refuse to hold the emotion in. (Do not send it to the person.) Or, if you want to be physical, you can throw socks at the wall as you scream about a frustration. You can hit a punching bag or run as you vent. With these types of venting tactics, you do not vent on anyone else. You are simply releasing it from yourself. If it is physical, like throwing socks or hitting a punching bag, you do not imagine that you are hitting anyone—you are just getting the emotion out. As you expend the energy, mentally imagine that you are releasing the negativity by simply thinking something like, "I refuse to hold this in—I am letting this go!"

Venting in this way hurts no one! So there is no guilt. There is no bitterness. And there are no repercussions.

The Brush Technique

This is a somewhat silly technique, but it can still be highly effective. Negative energy can be like cheddar cheese popcorn—it tends to stick to you. So after you have had a negative experience with someone, simply stand up and symbolically brush off your body. Imagine that you are brushing the negativity off of you, and refuse to let that person hurt or drain you with their negative energy.

Talking to Someone Who Cares

Sometimes, it helps to share your fears or stress with another human being who cares. Just make sure you are venting instead of being negative. As mentioned earlier, the difference between the two comes in intent and duration. You vent with the intent of release, and it has a finite duration. Negativity tends to recycle the pain and has no end in sight. Make sure you pick the right person and not someone who will ignore your emotions or make them worse. Pick someone who is caring but calm and a good sounding board. Also, tell them in advance what you want. Do you want them just to listen and care, or do you want advice? Sometimes, with good intentions, people can give you advice, even when you just want to be heard. That said, if venting is not helping you let it go, you might want to be open to some sound advice on solving your issue.

Journaling

Many people benefit from journaling their feelings. A journal is basically a diary in which you write down your thoughts, emotions, and events that you are experiencing. Another form of journaling that we mention elsewhere in this book is not journaling about problems but about what is right in your life, the things for which you are grateful. Even if you choose to journal about the stressful things, you might want to end with a few words about the blessed things in your life.

Worry Chair

The worry chair strategy is very useful for people with insomnia or who wake up and start worrying about their day. It is highly intrusive and not fun to do, but it is also highly effective. Psychologists have used this technique for decades to help people get control of their stress and lack of sleep.

Step 1: Set up a specific chair in your house that is designated as the
worry chair.

Step 2: If you are worrying about things and unable to sleep for more
than ten minutes, get out of your bed and go sit in the worry chair.

Step 3: Allow yourself to worry all you want when you are in the chair.
Take each worry to its conclusion before you move to the next worry.

Step 4: Stay there as long as you need to (until you are done worrying).

Step 5: Return to bed.

Step 6: If you start worrying again, rinse and repeat! Go to your chair,
and repeat the process. Do not allow yourself to worry in any other
spot in the house.

Step 7 (optional): You can add journaling to your worry time if
that is helpful for you.

After practicing this for several days, you will condition your worry to that chair instead of your bed. It puts you in control of the worry rather than having the worry control you.

RECHARGING YOUR BATTERY

After you have been through stress, it is important to recharge the batteries. Again, there are many ways to do that, but here are a few of our favorites.

Spa

When you think of recharging, one of the first things you should consider (if you have the financial means) is going to a spa. Whether you go for a facial, pedicure, massage, or other service, a spa is a great sanctuary from the cares of the world and very recharging.

Music

Music affects us at a very primal level and can be a powerful recharger. Unfortunately, when most people are down and depressed, they tend to listen to sad music that matches their mood. What if, instead of matching your mood, you have a playlist that can change your mood? Consider building a playlist of songs that feed your spirit instead of depleting it!

Sleep

We know few people who claim that they get enough sleep. This is especially true for single moms or busy professionals who feel that the workload just never ends. You can recharge in lots of ways, but if you are not getting enough sleep, it will catch up with you (as your authors know firsthand).

Hobbies

People love their hobbies, and these activities can be very recharging. Here is a sample list of hobbies that can be good for your soul:

Gardening

Collecting things that remind you of positive things from your child-
     hood, such as stamps, comic books, rocks, magnifying glasses,
     dolls, etc.

Scrapbooking (especially photographs of good memories)

Cooking

Drawing or painting

Acting

Knitting

Fishing

There are many different hobbies that are relaxing and recharging. That said, we have found that many soft souls do not spend enough time in their hobbies. They can feel guilty for taking time for themselves and forget that they need to be balanced and recharged in order to help others at their highest capacity.

Regular Breaks

Many people under stress tend to get busier and try to work harder. They start skipping meals and failing to take breaks in their day. To simply walk away from your work, even for ten minutes, can help you get your energy and your mind in the right state.

Nature

Refreshing is the word we think of when we think of nature. There is beauty in every season if we look for it, and for some people, getting outdoors and communing with nature is the key to connecting with their spirits. Whether it is a simple walk around the neighborhood, heading out to a forest preserve, or planning a trip to go hiking, nature, when viewed in the right light, is a great recharger.

● ● ●

These are just a few ideas on how to recharge, but there are many more. The key is to know yourself and know what feeds your batteries and then to make sure you care enough about yourself to commit to these things.

STANDING UP FOR YOURSELF

So let's say that you are good at taking care of yourself, you have methods to destress, and you take time to recharge, but you are involved in relationships that are hurting you in some form. Sadly, there is no shortage of ways human beings can hurt one another. Whether it is an emotionally abusive situation at home or a boss or coworker who takes advantage of their kind spirits, soft souls must learn how to draw boundaries in their lives if they are going to live with energy and joy. Unfortunately, many soft souls wait until the pain has built to a breaking point before they express themselves, and then their emotions come out as anger, aggression, or so dramatically that the soft souls then feel guilty or are distracted from the real issues with their levels of emotion. Many soft souls despise conflict and will avoid it at all costs. However, disagreements are part of life and, in fact, are a *critical* part of life. A relationship without conflict is a relationship without passion! If you are a passionate person, you are going to have strong feelings and opinions, and that is absolutely OK. Good, respectful, and healthy conflict creates greater creativity, better solutions, and, when done well, closer relationships. Avoidance of conflict creates lack of change and poorer solutions and becomes a wedge that prevents relationships from being as authentic and close as they can be.

There are many good books on setting boundaries and having disagreements, such as *When I Say No, I Feel Guilty* by Manuel J. Smith, *Boundaries: When to Say Yes, How to Say No to Take Control of Your Life* by Henry Cloud and John Townsend, and *The Coward's Guide to Conflict* by Tim Ursiny. But here are a few steps for setting boundaries in a way that will let you feel proud, confident, and strong.

Step One: Prepare for the Discussion

Ideally, take some time to do this, or if you have to do it on the spot, do it quickly.

Check for safety. How safe is it to have this conversation? In extreme cases such as physical abuse, you should reach out to expert sources for advice. On the other end of the spectrum, make sure you are not exaggerating the danger of the discussion.

Assess your rights. What rights would you give to a friend in the very same situation?

Check your energy. Are you able to approach the conflict with strength and the goal of resolution, or have you let it build up and you are just going to vent on the other person? Use venting techniques that we talked about earlier if you need to let off some steam first.

Picture the ideal resolution to the discussion. What do you want as a result of having the conversation? What does success look like? Enter the conversation with that positive goal in mind.

If you feel angry, check to see what you feel beneath the anger. Many times, anger is a protective device for softer feelings like hurt, disappointment, embarrassment, etc. Unfortunately, many people respond to anger with defensiveness. You will increase the odds of a positive resolution by going to the softer emotion and sharing that feeling. This sounds easy but can make you feel very vulnerable, so many people cover up their softer emotion with anger.

Step Two: Share Your Feelings or Perspectives

Be able to express your feelings with clarity. "When _____ happens, I feel _____."

Avoid accusations. Try to stay away from "you" statements like "You make me feel angry." These usually create defensiveness.

Step Three: Ask about Others' Feelings and Perspectives

Show interest in what others feel and think. Make statements and ask questions like "That is how I see it. That said, I also want to understand how you see it." Or "What are your feelings or thoughts about that?"

Try to reflect. Whether you agree or not, attempt to summarize what you hear to make sure you understand.

Step Four: Find Some Point of Agreement

Be genuine in your agreement. We have found that if you get someone talking long enough, it is easy to find some point of agreement. Make sure the point of agreement is authentic and powerful, saying something like "Where I completely agree with you is _____." Find as many points as possible.

Avoid the "but." If you listen to people argue, you will hear the word *but* come up frequently. *But* is a combative word and is perceived as "I don't believe anything I said before. Here is what I really think." So lose the *but* and replace it with *and*, *also*, *in addition*, *another way to view it*, etc. These will work much better to help you come to some point of agreement and action.

Step Five: Make a Request/Set a Boundary

Make sure others know what you want. Conflict where we basically spew all of our emotion on another human being rarely ends well. Have a concrete request in mind, and state it clearly.

Check on agreement. Make sure that you have agreement with your request or have a negotiated request that they commit to doing.

Ask for their requests. Make sure you show humility and ask what you could do better also. Just make sure these are in addition to your request, not in place of it.

When necessary, set a firm boundary like we mentioned in chapter 4, such as "We would be glad to come visit you for the holidays and hope we have a great time together. At the same time, I need you to know that if we feel like a lot of negative conflict starts happening, we will need to leave and return home."

Step Six: Repeat

Have multiple discussions. Accept the fact that habits are hard to change and one discussion may not fix the issue. Commit to having continued discussion until you get a change.

Remind them of previous discussions. If someone is not changing, go back to the fact that you have had this discussion before, and ask them what is getting in the way of changing how you are interacting together. See if you can problem-solve a solution.

Know that there is a time to escalate. We mentioned earlier that you improve your odds by going to the softer emotion rather than anger. That said, if you continue to not get any response when sharing the softer emotions, there are occasions where some people need to see your anger and will only respond to that intensity of emotion (though there is rarely a time when you should go to the intensity first). Also be willing to execute the consequence of crossing your boundary when needed.

While most soft souls (with the exception of those with the Fighter adaptation) do not enjoy conflict, even the mildest of souls can learn how to stand up for themselves in a way that is gentle, strong, and effective. If your soul is soft and the world seems harsh to you, we hope that you have found something in this chapter that will help you protect and recharge your spirit.

Conflict can be seen as a gift of energy, in which neither side loses and a new dance is created.

—*Thomas Crum*

CHAPTER 19

HOPE: THE ANTIDOTE FOR DESPAIR

When sorrows like sea billows roll;

Whatever my lot,

Thou has taught me to say

It is well, it is well, with my soul.

— Horatio Spafford, "It Is Well with My Soul"

THE HYMN "IT IS WELL WITH MY SOUL" WAS WRITTEN IN 1873 BY A CHICAGO lawyer named Horatio Spafford. The song evokes a powerful sense of peace in those who have heard it, but the story behind this song is anything but peaceful. Spafford was a man who experienced a harsh world. He was heavily invested in Chicago real estate, all of which was destroyed by the Great Chicago Fire of 1871. This happened just a year after his only son died at the age of four from scarlet fever. He knew that he, his wife, and their four daughters needed to get away for a while, so he planned an excursion from New York to Great Britain on the French steamer *Ville du Havre*.

At the last minute, Spafford had to delay his trip to deal with a business situation, so he sent his family along in advance. He was planning to join them as soon as his situation would allow. Nine days after his wife and daughters set sail, he received a telegram from his wife, informing him that she alone survived the trip. The *Ville du Havre* had collided with another vessel, and the accident took the lives of 226 people, including Spafford's four daughters. Spafford got on another ship to join his wife, and in the midst of his despair (and while on the ship and near the spot where his daughters died), he wrote this song of the peace that only comes from leaning into God. We can only imagine what he was truly feeling, but we suspect that his comfort came from the hope that his daughters were in a better place and that he would one day see them again.

THE POWER OF HOPE

Despair comes in many forms. It is easy to lose hope when life has beaten you down. Multiple losses, betrayals, hurt feelings, etc. can lead even the strongest of soft souls to wonder *Is this worth it?* or *Will life ever get better?* If you have ever asked these questions, you are not alone. The antithesis of despair is hope, and hope can also come in many forms. You can hope that things will get better. You can hope that there is meaning in your struggle. You can hope that there is something bigger than what we experience on this planet. The mind-set you have around your struggles will highly impact whether you land on despair or on hope.

Years ago, at a popular amusement park, there was a game we often played. A balloon was placed on top of a plastic clown head, and players would use a water pistol to squirt water into the clown's mouth. This created pressure, and whoever popped the balloon on the top of the clown's head first would be a winner. We eventually learned how you could win that game every time (as long as you were a decent shot). The secret to winning was to sit in the chair of the previous winner. The reason this strategy was so effective was that, since the previous winner burst the balloon, the park worker would put a new balloon on the clown's head. The other balloons would expand and contract, while the new balloon had never experienced pressure. The old balloons could withstand more pressure because they had been stretched. The new balloon could not handle the same level of pressure and would burst. So when it comes to having despair or having hope, some of it depends on if you see yourself as a new balloon or an old balloon. Have you been through a lot in life? Have you navigated tough times? Have you made it through the most atrocious of circumstances? If so, then maybe you are an old balloon; maybe everything in life has made you able to handle all of the challenges that come your way! If you think of yourself as a new balloon, you think, *I can't handle any more pain or stress!* If you think of yourself as an experienced, seasoned, old balloon, you are going to think, *After all I have been through, there is nothing I can't handle!*

One key to hope is to see everything that you have gone through in life as part of who you are. While some things may be ugly, you still honor them as components on your path that have made you the wonderful, beautiful human being that you have become. Use everything you have experienced to make you stronger, wiser, and even more adaptive. Derive hope from all that you have survived and overcome! Find meaning in every experience you have had in life. Honor every emotion, decision, and event as part of who you are. And in the end, realize that there is something bigger than all of us. Despair cannot withstand the light and power of hope.

Alexandre Dumas wrote, "There is neither happiness nor misery in the world; there is only the comparison of one state with another, nothing more. He who has felt the deepest grief is best able to experience supreme happiness." We believe that these words contain great wisdom, as the soft soul who has most deeply felt the harshness of the world is also most able to experience the joy and wonder of the world. By surviving the rough patches in life, you can more appreciate the good moments, the kind words, the great times of your life. By understanding loss, you can also understand and appreciate more of what you do have. The person who grew up poor can often feel more gratitude later in life if they have some financial success. The person who was abused in the past can (if they overcome their fears) feel the greatest of appreciation for a spouse who treats them kindly and gently. By seeing your difficulties as a comparison that allows you to love more, appreciate more, feel more, you find some meaning in your struggles and can see them as an important part of what has made you the wonderful person that you are today.

Some find hope in seeing their struggles as temporary. If we know anything about life, we know that it will eventually change. It does not stay the same. Many struggles are not truly permanent. (Of course, if you believe in the afterlife of heaven, then no struggles are permanent.) We build hope by seeing our troubles as temporary and knowing that at some moment in the future, things could be better.

Others find hope by making sure that they don't let the good things in life be overshadowed by the bad things. Some people have the amazing ability to be grateful for the smallest of things in life, even when they are going through tough times. They are able to compartmentalize the bad things in life as just one aspect of their existence rather than falling into the "everything is horrible" mind-set. Gratitude is a powerful force and is great protection against despair.

I Hope

The Shawshank Redemption is a powerful movie about the enduring power of hope. It is a story about a banker who is falsely convicted of a double homicide and sentenced to a life in prison. In the movie, Andy (played by Tim Robbins) befriends another convict named Red (played by Morgan Freeman). Andy and

Red have differing views on the role of hope in prison. Several scenes in the movie capture how they view and we can view hope (spoiler alert).

In one scene, Andy is talking about the beauty of music. "They can't get that from you. Haven't you ever felt that way about music?" he asks Red, who says, "I played a mean harmonica as a younger man. Lost interest in it though. Didn't make much sense in here." Andy argues that it makes the most sense in their situation so that they don't forget that "there are places in this world that aren't made out of stone. That there's something inside…that they can't get to, that they can't touch. That's yours." He is, of course, referring to hope. Red gets irritated and talks about hope as a dangerous thing that can drive you insane.

Some people refuse to hope, because they want to avoid the disappointment that can occur if the thing you hope for does not happen. Sadly, this will rob you of the wonderful excitement that hope can bring. You deprive yourself of pleasure in order to avoid potential pain. This seems to be Red's mind-set at this part of the movie.

In one of the most powerful scenes, Andy gets released from solitary confinement only to discover that the one man who could prove his innocence has been murdered. As he and Red sit in the prison yard, Andy talks about what he is going to do when he gets out of prison (which seems impossible at this point). He talks about going to a small fishing village in Mexico called Zihuatanejo. As he dreams about the life he would build there and how Red could join him, Red, out of good intentions, tries to get his friend to stop hoping. He calls Andy's vision a "pipe dream" and pleads with him to stop doing this to himself. Finally, Andy ends their debate and says to Red that it comes down to a simple choice: "Get busy living, or get busy dying." As Andy walks off, he has Red promise him that if he ever gets out of prison, he will go to a specific field and retrieve something from that field. Red agrees.

At this point in the movie, you don't know Andy's plan, and the movie hints that Andy may be suicidal and that despair has won over hope (again, spoiler alert). We worry that Andy may be getting busy dying. As the story dramatically unfolds, we find instead that Andy escapes from prison and heads to Mexico. He got busy living.

Red is happy for his friend but deeply misses the hope that Andy had brought into his life. Paradoxically, Red is finally released from prison when he accepts his fate and quits trying to change it. He gets a job at a grocery store but finds that he hates life on the outside and that his fear is tempting him to commit a crime in order to return to prison, a life he knows. However, he remembers his promise to Andy that if he ever got free, he would go to that field in the country to find something that Andy had placed there. Red goes to the field and discovers money plus a letter written by Andy after he escaped prison on how to find him in Mexico. In the letter, Andy writes, "Remember, Red, hope is a good thing, maybe the best of things, and no good thing ever dies."

Red overcomes his fears and decides to go find Andy. In this final scene as he travels to Mexico, we hear Red's voice saying, "I find I'm so excited that I can barely sit still or hold a thought in my head. I think it's the excitement only a free man can feel. A free man at a start of a long journey whose conclusion is uncertain. I hope I can make it across the border. I hope to see my friend and shake his hand. I hope the Pacific is as blue as it has been in my dreams. I hope."

Our journeys are uncertain. And while we don't completely control the outcome, we can control our choices. We have a choice to see hope as a good thing that never dies, we have a choice to get busy living, and we have a choice to turn fear into excitement and risk disappointment as we hope for our future. We hope these words speak to you. We hope that if you are ever disappointed, you embrace that as the natural emotion you feel when you don't get what you want and don't allow it to destroy your hope. We hope your journey is exciting. We hope.

WHEN SELF-HELP DOESN'T HELP

So where does your hope come from? Do you find meaning in your struggles that gives you hope? Do you guard your mind and make sure you see your struggles as temporary? Do you focus on what is good in your life despite the struggles? Do you find hope in a power bigger than you?

Your authors obviously believe in the power of psychological tools to help navigate this harsh world and find comfort and belief. That said, for some, self-help just isn't enough. It can be a Band-Aid or temporary relief, but the pain never goes away, and life as you experience it never seems to get better. If you feel this way, we only have one suggestion for you: lean into God.

While none of us should wait until we are desperate before we seek out our Creator, those who are in the deepest despair really have no choice; we must focus on faith. Faith is a critical part of how we deal with this difficult world, and we believe that faith is a necessary part of navigating this planet as a soft soul. Your authors believe that seeking truth and finding your personal faith is, in our experience, an essential part of the human struggle and one that should not be taken lightly. And while we certainly don't want to be arrogant and think we have all of the answers, we also want to be transparent about our faith and the role it has played in our soft souls. And while your authors do have some different beliefs from each other, the commonality of our beliefs that should be apparent by now is that we both do look to the Bible as our source of understanding our Creator. Our faith in God and in Jesus Christ has been critical in our survival of our own journey.

In fact, some of you have likely noticed that this book and our version of the different aspects of soft souls are loosely based on the beatitudes in the Bible. Here are words of wisdom far greater than ours:

Now when Jesus saw the crowds, he went up on a mountainside and sat down. His disciples came to him, and he began to teach them. He said:

Blessed are the poor in spirit, for theirs is the kingdom of heaven.

Blessed are those who mourn, for they will be comforted.

Blessed are the meek, for they will inherit the earth.

Blessed are those who hunger and thirst for righteousness, for they will be filled.

Blessed are the merciful, for they will be shown mercy.

Blessed are the pure in heart, for they will see God.

Blessed are the peacemakers, for they will be called children of God.

Blessed are those who are persecuted because of righteousness, for theirs is the kingdom of heaven.

—Matthew 5: 1–10, New International Version

We believe that the ultimate solution for the soft soul is to fall into the arms of God and find purpose in the life they are leading on this earth. While relationships can be helpful and an understanding of psychology can equip you with great tools, we have found that having a deep faith and a belief that God made you as a unique human being and has a purpose for your life is even more powerful. When you accept that, you can more easily love your life and celebrate your soft soul. And while we don't have all the answers, we do want to encourage you to seek, pray for truth, and explore your relationship with a power much bigger than your own.

I have been driven many times upon my knees by the overwhelming conviction that I had nowhere else to go. My own wisdom and that of all about me seemed insufficient for that day.

—*Abraham Lincoln*

Hope is the thing with feathers

That perches in the soul

And sings the tune without the words

And never stops at all.

—Emily Dickinson

PART FOUR:

REVISITING THE FAMILY OF SOFT SOULS

CHAPTER 20

WHERE ARE THEY NOW?

I am fundamentally an optimist. Whether that comes from nature or nurture,
I cannot say. Part of being optimistic is keeping one's head pointed toward
the sun, one's feet moving forward. There were many dark moments when my
faith in humanity was sorely tested, but I would not and could not give myself
up to despair. That way lays defeat and death.

—Nelson Mandela

At the time of this writing, it has been twelve years since Christi's death. While their stories are ongoing and may have many more twists, changes, and surprises, we want to end our journey with you by catching up on the lives of our family of soft souls.

THE IDEALIST

"I still love *our* little girl..." Frances takes a long breath and repeats God's message again and again in her soul. It gives her comfort. The memories of her daughter's last week of life, memories of how she gave her soft soul, broken and tarnished by the world, meekly back to God inspire her continued faith. Frances has been merciful to her father, merciful to her husband, merciful to her wayward child. They are forgiven for any harms they caused her. She feels that God has rewarded her mercy by giving her little girl mercy beyond measure. Despite Christi's rebellion, He took her home to be with Him, and Frances finds comfort in the fact that her meek little girl is free of pain and is safe. God's overwhelming grace drives her to seek His face in every moment, to seek His wisdom, to lay everything in her life in His hands. She does not worry about her other children or fret over the welfare of her grandchildren. She knows that God is in control and that with Him, even death does not mean the end. Frances is more grateful now than ever for the sacrifice of Jesus.

She is well into her seventies, and her body suffers from a neurological disorder that has left her barely able to walk, but Frances will not allow the devil to win. She sits at a small table on her back porch, fervently studying God's words each day, exploring the causes of addiction, counseling friends and family by phone. She teaches her grandchildren and her great-granddaughter about God's love, and she is greatly honored and favored for the mercy she has shown them as they struggle to do God's will. She sees her meek little lamb in all of their faces, and it makes her heart fill with joy.

At Christmas, she taught her great-granddaughter about Jesus, and at only five, her little great-granddaughter said, "Oh, Meme, I want Jesus in my heart." Frances knows that a single moment sitting with her great-grandmother on the floor, reading a picture book about Jesus's birth, has changed her great-granddaughter's destiny forever. She is filled with awe and wonder.

Someday, Frances dreams she will find a way to start homes of love and healing in honor of Christi's struggle. It is the greatest desire of her heart, and though it seems impossible given her age and health, even now, she is an Idealist. She guides her son Paul on his journey to start a mission to help addicts or other people who need the Lord. She tries to help him know when to fight and which battles are most important. So many useless battles can be fought when a loved one is addicted, but the one true battle against addiction's darkness is fought with the weapons of prayer, trust, and supplication to God.

She still longs to walk freely again. She prepares herself in faith and hopes to actively serve God once more, never realizing how many people she helps daily, there on that little porch.

THE FIGHTER

Paul puts down the phone after his regular Sunday call with his mother. He has just returned from working on his new church, a church his father once preached in. He found it abandoned in the country near his land and petitioned for the right to use it. Only three people came this Sunday, but he is excited and cannot wait to share what they talked about with his mom. His dogs bark in the background, and he looks around his cabin. His room is full of pictures of family. Of all of his siblings, Paul is the most nostalgic. He believes in honoring the dead by keeping their memories alive and mourns every anniversary of every death. Despite the fact that it has been decades since Ken died, Paul tears up when he reads the poem he wrote after his father's death:

Lord, I praise you for my father with a body small and frail.
I know that you will hold him; even though all of us fail.
I had my time to hold him; now he's yours forevermore.
Let me remember that special time,
As he goes in your hands, not mine.
Be with him on his journey; keep him safe and warm.
Let him talk to Saint Paul; let him ask about the thorn.
I know he was one of yours, Lord; He praised your holy name.
Now be with us as we go on,
As he goes in your hands, not mine.

Paul is so grateful that God has used him to help others. For a period of his life, he felt removed from God as though he could not really lean on Him for anything. These days, he knows that the Lord is the only solution for the pain of the world and loves to share that with other people. He knows in his heart that every trial, every battle, every hurt he has experienced has prepared him for serving God.

Paul lives on a large piece of land surrounded by trees, water, and wildlife. He built his log cabin with his own two hands. He loves to lie down on the ground at night, listening to the wind flowing through the trees. He enjoys the three hours it takes to mow his lawn. He relaxes by swimming in his creek. He loves resting in his bed, listening to the rain hitting the roof that he built. He even takes pleasure at deer hissing at him as they pass by. He is content. He has some physical challenges, but Paul is not one to whine about them. He accepts and loves his life and yet does not fear dying. He has a trust and confidence in God to both take care of him on this planet and to welcome him into heaven when his time is done.

His life now is not like the life he had the first time he escaped to the land. During those previous years, he mostly kept to himself; now, he reaches out often to help people trapped in the same darkness he has experienced. He has met many such people in a Salvation Army shelter much like the one in which his little sister passed away. He thinks about the musical performance he recently gave there, about the video of his sister and her kids, about the picture of his sister in her casket. He thinks about the faces of the newly sober people in the audience. Did he get through to any of them? He has kept his sister's memory alive. He prays he has changed the men there and that they will not fall to death from their addictions as his sister did. He still cries when he tells her story, even though it has been twelve years. Paul, though he is a fighter, truly has a soft soul.

His heart is less about fighting others and more about fighting for others. A few years ago, he noticed a captain at the Salvation Army shelter who seemed deeply saddened on Christmas. Paul found out that the man had been separated from his family in his own struggle with addiction. Now sober and serving God, he had been unable to find them. Paul was so moved that he immediately began the search. He picked up the phone and called his little sister Jamie. Both were amazed by the way God moved and performed miracles to help them find and reunite this family. It reunited Paul with his sister as well.

The captain's family had believed he was dead, and when they heard their son was alive, they were shocked and overjoyed. Paul was bursting with emotion as he drove seventy-eight miles to tell his friend that he had found his family. It was not God's will for any family to be so shattered, and Paul smiled as the captain got on the phone and talked with his mother for the first time in thirty-five years. Paul's hunger to bring justice, to put in right standing that which had been torn apart, was filled, and it gave him the sense that he was fulfilling the mission his father had been unable to complete. The devil was losing, and as a fighter, nothing satisfied Paul more.

Paul looks around his land, at the cabins that need to be repaired and the dreams he has for the place. It is moving so slowly, but he knows that God had to rebuild him first. He hates the idea of his soul being soft in any way, but he reluctantly accepts it. He was born to hunger and thirst for God's righteousness, to fight God's battle, and he submits his soul to be softened for that purpose.

THE PLEASER

Tim stares into the woods behind his house as he drinks a glass of Cabernet Sauvignon and remembers the dreams of his youth. It has been over twenty-seven years since the death of his father, and much has happened. He graduated with a PhD and was in private practice as a therapist for seven years, but his failure to fully deal with his past up to that point caused that world to explode. Tim's second career and the last nineteen years have been highly successful. He has written books, has been interviewed on television and radio, travels the world, and makes a good living. He has been blessed with a wonderful family. His wife loves her life, and his kids are happy and stable and have loving hearts. He adores his three boys with all of his heart, and they adore him. All three of his sons are different, and all three bring him joy in different ways. His wife is beautiful (but too humble to realize how beautiful she is), and she loves him very much. He loves it when she laughs. He loves how she is obsessed with Disney

World. He loves how they have navigated decades of challenges and yet still remain married and still love each other deeply.

As he takes another sip of his wine, he wonders why he still feels sadness on occasion. He has been so blessed; what right does he have to feel sad? He knows that part of his pain comes from the standards he sets for himself and his inability to fully keep them. He knows part of his sadness comes from his past and mistakes he has made. He despises hurting people, and his past imperfection can haunt him. He wants to heal, never hurt. Tim has always been one to want peace and harmony between people. Tim wants to continue to grow in his ability to be more selfless. It is a mission. He wants to continually learn from the past and keep growing.

Several years ago, Tim decided to do something to make the child inside himself happy. As he turned fifty, he was reflecting on the simple question "What have I wanted to do in life that I have not accomplished?" The only thing that came to him went back to his love of comics. He wanted to write a comic book and pitched the following to Marvel Comics:

> *Synopsis: A teenage boy named Zachary, who is living in poverty, a broken home, and a troubled environment, is about to jump off his roof and kill himself. As he is about to step off the ledge, he is hit by a piece of debris from a fight on an opposing roof. As he recovers, he stands up to see Captain America battling overwhelming odds (Hydra or some equivalent) on an opposing rooftop. Despite the impossible odds, Cap refuses to give up. At a pivotal moment, Zachary is able to distract the villains, which enables Cap to turn the tide of the battle. After a thankful salute*

from Cap, Zachary returns to his apartment and picks up the phone. He is calling a suicide hotline and says the only words that will appear in the story: "I need help."

The story was symbolic of Tim's own life and captured the depression and helplessness that often leads to suicide. The editors liked the story, and it was soon published. Tim was allowed to use the real number for the suicide hotline, and this led to a significant amount of press for the story. Message boards were lit up with people talking about the story and their own struggles. What started as a simple bucket-list item for a nerdy dream led to an event that possibly saved lives. Tim was pleased. He was powerless as a child, but not as an adult.

So at times, Tim feels sadness, but most of the time, he lives in gratitude. He is so thankful for his life, his family, and his friends. Yes, most of the time, he is happy, feels blessed, and is trying to enjoy every moment in his life. And while Tim can be hard on himself, he knows that in the end, life is not like the comic books. It is not that simple. It is not that clean. His father did hurtful things, and yet he was loving, fun, and, at his core, a man who loved God. His sister hurt so many people, and her addiction made her a shell of who she used to be, and yet, in her sober moments, she felt very guilty. She could also be kind, compassionate, and full of spark. He thinks of his own life, the good he has done and the bad he has done. He hopes that the good outweighs the bad and is grateful for the grace he has received for the mistakes he has made. These days, he truly tries to live up to the person his wife and children deserve. As he takes another sip of Cabernet, he has this thought: *Perhaps there is no such thing as a villain or a hero. Perhaps we are all just human.*

THE INVISIBLE ONE

She is tired this morning. Jamie is tired almost every day, but at least the house is quiet for a while. She looks at her son asleep on the couch, his long, thin body hanging over the edges. She thinks about the struggles he has had—the sensory issues, the phobias, and the anxieties. He has overcome so much. She prays she is enough for him. It is hard to resist the urge to kiss his tan cheeks, but she resists because, like Christi, he is a grump when he is wakened. To him, Jamie is his mom and always has been, and though he did not come from her body, in her soul, she knows that God always meant him to be hers. He even has her birthmark. Christi had fulfilled her desire to give her sister a child, not just one but three. For that, Jamie will love her for eternity, despite what her sister's addiction had stolen from her.

As for Christi's girls, they still struggle. Their soft souls hurting, they search for something to ease the pain. Like all of us, sometimes they hit the mark and sometimes they miss it. Their mother, in her guilt and feelings of failure, thought they would be fine without her. Twelve years later, they both still grieve. But both have beautiful loving hearts that long to make the world a kinder, easier place for others to exist. They share their compassion and the hard lessons they have learned behind a beauty shop chair where even strangers feel welcome to tell their life stories and where the girls bring out their inner and outer beauty. Hair was their mother's love. She spent hours on hers and wouldn't leave the house until it was perfect, and they honor her with every hairstyle. She would be so proud of them! She IS proud of them.

Jacki has made Jamie a grandmother to a vivacious little girl with a vibrant personality like her mother's. Hunter Nicole has changed her mother. The soft soul that Jacki had hidden away at just three years old pours out on her child, her little brother, her grandmother, and her aunt. She has become tenderhearted though she will adamantly deny it if you say so!

Samantha's soft soul has had a tougher time. She has suffered many great losses and the pain can, at times, feel unbearable. But Samantha knows who her Creator created her to be. She remembers the little girl who was a "light" in the midst of sorrow and she fights daily to return to being that light. She is strong and she is determined. Samantha knows where the source of help is. She pushes to love beyond her brokenness and reaches out to people that no one else seems to care about.

As for their aunt, she has learned not to worry. Jamie no longer attempts to control the situation around her or to try to make people go on the path that will save them from inflicting more harm. She has learned not to step into a role that belongs to her children's Creator. She reminds herself of these words from the concentration camp survivor Corrie Ten Boom: "I have held many things in my hands, and I have lost them all, but whatever I have placed in God's hands, that, I still possess."

So Jamie prays. She prays with all she has left in her tired spirit, and she is waiting on the Lord.

The phone rings. It is Tim. Jamie feels comfort when she hears his voice. He is still her best friend as he was in childhood. Tim has an idea, a project for them to do together that would be good for his heart and good for her life. She is intrigued by the idea, but she wonders if she is up to the task; she doubts her talent and fears failing. Tim reassures her; he believes in her and feels they can do something deep and meaningful if they work together. She agrees, and they say their usual "luv ya." It is something they all do now. They don't leave each other without saying it, because they all wish desperately they had time to say it once more to their little sister.

God has given Jamie the greatest desire of her life. Her children are blessed, healthy, and close to God. Ashamed, she admits she still longs for more. She still longs to create something that will touch others' souls. She longs for the artist inside of her, who is separate from mother, daughter, and caretaker. She ponders if she will ever find her personal destiny, if she will again find the passion inside her soul to be able to act, to paint, to create, and, most of all, if she can ever return to her first love, which was to write.

With a prayer and fighting her deepest insecurities, she places her fingers on her laptop keyboard. As her hesitant fingers stroke the keys, she begins to write this book.

To accomplish great things, we must not only act, but also dream; not only plan, but also believe.

—Anatole France

ADDITIONAL RESOURCES

For additional resources to encourage your soul, go to www.softsouls.com.

OTHER BOOKS
BY YOUR AUTHORS

The Coach's Handbook: Exercises for Resolving Conflict in the Workplace by Tim
Ursiny, PhD

Coaching the Sale by Tim Ursiny, PhD, and Gary DeMoss with Jim Morel

The Confidence Plan: How to Build a Stronger You by Tim Ursiny, PhD

The Coward's Guide to Conflict by Tim Ursiny, PhD

The Top Performer's Guide to Attitude by Tim Ursiny, PhD, Gary DeMoss, and Marc
Ybaben, PhD

The Top Performer's Guide to Change by Tim Ursiny, PhD, and Barbara A. Kay, MA

The Top Performer's Guide to Conflict by Tim Ursiny, PhD, and Dave Bolz

The Top Performer's Guide to Speeches and Presentations by Tim Ursiny, PhD, and
Gary DeMoss with Jim Morel

Tough Times Tactics: A Brief Practical Guide to De-stressing, Recharging and Focusing by
Tim Ursiny, PhD, and Carole Cowperthwaite-O'Hagan, RCC

ABOUT THE AUTHORS

TIM URSINY, PHD, CBC, RCC

Dr. Tim Ursiny is the CEO and founder of Advantage Coaching & Training Inc. (www.advantagecoaching.com). He is a speaker and certified business coach specializing in helping individuals reach peak performance and life satisfaction. He received his undergraduate degree from Wheaton College and his doctorate in psychology from Northern Illinois University. He has written or co-written multiple books, including *The Confidence Plan*, *The Top Performer's Guide to Attitude*, and *The Coward's Guide to Conflict*, which is in its fourth printing and has been translated into multiple foreign languages. Tim is a frequent speaker on a variety of topics that benefit individuals in the workplace and in their personal lives. He is a frequent speaker for Fortune 100 companies and enjoys coaching individuals and teams. Tim has been interviewed and appeared in the *Wall Street Journal*, the *Bottom Line*, the *Chicago Tribune*, *People Magazine*, *Reader's Digest*, *First for Women*, and other periodicals. He has also appeared on *CNN Radio News*, *VH-1 News*, *Total Living*, and *ABC Channel 7 News*. Currently, Tim lives in Wheaton, IL, with his wife of thirty-four years and their youngest son.

JAMIE URSINY, MIT

Jamie Ursiny is a former elementary school teacher, teen counselor, and graduate of the University of North Carolina's master of instructional technology program. Jamie's experiences working with battered women and children have developed her perspective of the path to healing. Jamie temporarily retired from her work with other children and families to raise her special needs son adopted after her sister's death. Jamie is currently working on a grant to create a special needs play museum for children like her son. In her master's training, Jamie co-developed projects for a local women's services organization to help women deal with anger issues, created an online course for the parents of children with sensory processing disorder, and headed the project design for a sobriety ranch named after her sister. She is an amateur filmmaker and photographer, as well as a Christian web designer in training. Jamie is a resident of North Carolina. She maintains a close supportive relationship with her deceased sister's older daughters and grandchild.